Hope for the
TROUBLED HEART

The Journey to an Untroubled Heart

by Dennis Kizziar
with James Lund

WESTBOW
PRESS®
A DIVISION OF THOMAS NELSON
& ZONDERVAN

WestBow Press books may be ordered through booksellers or by contacting:

WestBow Press
A Division of Thomas Nelson & Zondervan
1663 Liberty Drive
Bloomington, IN 47403
www.westbowpress.com
844-714-3454

ISBN: 978-1-4497-1519-9 (sc)
ISBN: 978-1-4497-1520-5 (hc)

Library of Congress Control Number: 2011925893

Print information available on the last page.

Cover image: Photos.com, Jupiter Images
Cover design: Jody Conners
Interior design: Ellen Steele

WestBow Press rev. date: 4/11/2011

THE PATHWAY THROUGH LIFE

The image on the cover was chosen because that pathway is much like the one on which we journey through life. As believers, our view of the path ahead is often limited and sometimes obscure, while at other times we see it clearly. Sometimes the path winds up and down—the highs and lows of life. Sometimes there are seemingly insurmountable mountains and nearly endless valleys. The valleys can be places of refreshment or can fill us with fear and anxiety. Sometimes the path is rocky or filled with potholes; at other times it's smooth. But one thing we know for sure, whatever the path is like and wherever it leads: Someone has gone ahead of us on that path. God always shines His light in front of us to guide each step, whether it's a baby step or a giant stride. That light gives us hope to keep moving forward because He is there with us, holding us up and giving us strength. If we keep our eyes focused on that light, we will find that renewed strength and hope which enables us to choose to enjoy the journey, no matter what we encounter along the way. May this book help you embrace your journey with the Lord to an untroubled heart.

DEDICATION

This book is dedicated with deep gratitude and love to my wife, Joan. She, apart from my salvation, has without a doubt been God's greatest gift to me.

God has also blessed me with many wonderful friends who have been a tremendous source of encouragement and support during a time of great difficulty in my life. I wish I could name all of them but you know who you are and God certainly knows who you are. Each of you has my profound thanks. May God encourage you and reward you for the significant part you have had in ministering to me.

Four incredibly faithful friends who played a vital role in my healing and restoration and deserve special mention are Keith and Charlotte Brewer and Ray and Donna Settelmeyer. They have continually shown me unconditional love, held out hope, provided godly guidance, and were and are powerful demonstrations of His amazing grace to me. Without them this book would never have been written. Thanks for never giving up on me and always being there for me. You are the best!

Lastly and most importantly, I give praise and thanks to the God of all grace. I dedicate this book and my life to Him for the furtherance of His Kingdom.

Dennis Kizziar
Bend, Oregon
September 2008

CONTENTS

Introduction

I see it when I preach. I can tell by the way men and women lean forward as I describe the promises of love and peace found in the Gospel. It's in the longing in their eyes.

I see it when I meet one-on-one with people to counsel them. As they pour out their problems and worries, I find myself nodding in recognition.

I've seen it when I look in the mirror. I've had it too.

"It" is a troubled heart, and in so many ways it's the face of Christianity today.

By their own admission, an increasing number of believers are not experiencing the joy and life-change offered by Jesus Christ. Instead, they are frustrated and disillusioned. Their marriages are deteriorating; their relationships with their kids are marked by chaos and conflict; they're giving in to self-destructive behaviors. The Christian life simply isn't working for them. Many of these people are settling for mediocrity by covering up their problems with a happy face. An alarming number are giving up on Christianity altogether.

Have I just described your life? Have you become a better actor instead of a better Christian? Is your heart so heavy and confused that you're secretly ready to abandon your faith?

And yet Jesus said, "Do not let your heart be troubled, neither let it be afraid—stop allowing yourselves to be agitated and disturbed; and do not permit yourselves to be fearful and intimidated and cowardly and unsettled" (John 14:27 AMP).

"Do not let." "Do not permit." Was Jesus really implying that we can do something about our bewilderment and frustration, that we have the power to change? Inspired by a gradual awakening to the state of my own troubled heart, I've spent the last few years exploring that very question. And I've made a vital discovery: Each of us *can* live with an untroubled heart—a heart marked by God's joy and peace, a heart that has been changed, freed, healed, and renewed. We've missed it because we've failed to get to the heart of the matter.

Keep reading and I'll explain what I mean.

CHAPTER ONE

A TROUBLED HEART

"O Sovereign Lord, deal well with me for your name's sake; out
of the goodness of your love, deliver me. For I am poor and needy, and
my heart is wounded within me."

PSALM 109:21–22

I was nineteen years old and miserable. I'd spent most of my high school years partying and fighting, and had barely graduated. For the previous year I'd worked in a warehouse in Oakland, California. Finally, after twelve months of packing boxes, I'd earned a vacation, so a friend and I celebrated by driving to Reno for several days of drinking and run-ins with the city police. In more ways than one, it was a wasted week.

Now I was at my grandparents' home in Turlock. It was Saturday afternoon; I had to be back at work in Oakland, ninety miles away, by Monday morning. I didn't know how I could face another year of box-packing. I was completely depressed, with no hopes or plans for the rest of my life—or even for that night.

Suddenly, an idea popped into my head. *Judy Barrows lives around here. I wonder if she'd go out with me tonight?*

My friend Richard had once dated Judy when we all lived in the area. I hardly knew her, but I remembered she was a pretty brunette. I looked up Judy's number and called. To my surprise, she accepted my short-notice date proposal.

A few hours later, I pulled up to Judy's ranch-style home in my pride and joy, a '53 green and yellow Chevy Bel Air. Judy, wearing a yellow summer dress, looked great. My hopes of quickly whisking her away in my dream mobile were soon dashed, however.

"Dennis, my brother is going to be on television in a few minutes," Judy said. "Would you mind if we watched a little of the program?"

What could I say? I reluctantly consented.

After family introductions, I sat down in the Barrows' living room with Judy and her father, mother, brother, and sister, wondering what I was getting myself into. The program host came on and announced that we were about to see a Billy Graham crusade from Madison Square Garden in New York.

I'd heard of Billy Graham, but didn't know anything about him. And I certainly didn't know until that moment that Cliff Barrows, the program's master of ceremonies and song leader, was Judy's brother!

We watched for a few minutes. I had no interest in the message or what Billy Graham was saying about the Bible. As far as I was concerned, church was for hypocrites and old ladies. I could feel my palms start to sweat. This was not what I had in mind for the evening.

Finally, I couldn't take it anymore. I turned to Judy and whispered, "Maybe it's time for us to go."

Her father heard me. "Dennis," he said, "I think it would be a good idea for you to watch the whole program." The look in his eye and the tone of his voice made it clear that the matter was not up for debate. If I wanted to date this man's daughter, I was going to have to sit through the entire program.

It was one of the longest hours of my life.

At last, the program ended. I barely remember where Judy and I went that night—probably to the local drive-in for something to eat. But I'll never forget what happened when we got back to her house.

We parked in Judy's driveway and started to talk. I shared about how much I disliked my warehouse job, described my awful "vacation," and admitted that my life had no meaning or direction.

Judy looked at me intently. "Dennis, you need what Billy was talking about tonight—a personal relationship with Jesus Christ."

I raised my hand. "Oh, no," I said. "I've already heard one sermon too many tonight. I don't need another one from you. I think I'd better get going."

"Okay," she answered. "But before you go, I want to pray for you." Judy didn't wait for me to answer. She closed her eyes and in a sweet, gentle voice, started praying out loud, inviting Jesus to move into and take hold of my life.

I was stunned. No one had ever prayed like this just for me.

When she finished, Judy opened her eyes and looked again at me. "Now," she said, "why don't *you* pray and give your life to Christ?"

The strangest feeling came over me. My resistance seemed to melt away. The desire to escape was gone. For some reason, I couldn't say no to Judy's question. Instead, I looked down and began to speak.

"God," I said in a low voice, "if You're really there and You're real…if You can do anything with this crazy life of mine…then do it."

For me, the experience was like being in a dark room and suddenly finding the light switch. I knew this was real. I'd met the Living Christ right there in Judy Barrows' driveway. I said good-bye to Judy, raced back to my grandparents' place, and woke up my grandmother.

"Grandma, you won't believe it," I said. "I accepted Jesus tonight. I'm a Christian!"

My grandmother, who'd been sleeping soundly and wasn't wearing her hearing aides, glasses, or false teeth, had some trouble getting my message. She thought I was drunk again.

"Go back to bed, Denny," she said. "You'll feel better in the morning."

I did feel better the next day—not because I was recovering from a hangover, but because I now had hope. I returned to Oakland, bought a Bible, and a few days later felt prompted to quit my job at the warehouse. I loaded my few possessions into the Bel Air and drove to Los Angeles, where I soon convinced the registrar at a Christian school then called Biola College to allow me to enroll. Biola was a new world to me, and I loved it. I soaked up the teaching there like a sponge.

I also came to appreciate the attributes of another student named Joan. I dated several girls at Biola, but when my eyes fell on Joan, I was captivated. I had never met anyone with the same measure of grace, beauty, quiet spirit, purity, godliness, and innocence. For some reason, she also seemed to see something in me. By the end of my four years at Biola, we were engaged to be married.

I was on my way to a great life, full of love for the Lord and excited about spending the rest of my days with my new wife, serving God, and spreading the message of Christ. The hopeless, drifting, self-destructive young man I'd been before was gone. I'd made a 180-degree turn. Now that I'd committed myself to Christ, I knew that my worries were over.

At least, that's what I thought at the time. What I didn't know was that down deep, in the hidden chambers of my heart, I was still very troubled.

VOMIT FROM THE HEART

Many of us begin our new lives as Christians with the secret expectation that everything will be different and that the rest of our days will be a pleasant stroll down Easy Street. And it's only after considerable experience, reflection on Scripture, and spiritual maturity that we begin to understand that the trials and troubles of daily life don't go away after we commit ourselves to Christ. Sometimes our problems even get worse. It was Peter, after all, who wrote, "Do not be surprised at the painful trial you are suffering, as though something strange were happening to you. But rejoice that you participate in the sufferings of Christ, so that you may be overjoyed when his glory is revealed" (1 Peter 4:12–13).

There are always challenges, events that plague us from without and threaten to do significant damage. This is part of life. God sometimes uses these trials to draw us closer to Him, and likewise our relationship with Jesus helps us deal with each unexpected crisis.

But there are also troubles that torment us from within. These are the kind that can cause the greatest harm. They are like time bombs waiting to go off. They are the weapons that Satan deploys most easily to destroy our lives and faith, and so many of us are blown away by the explosions.

I watched one of these bombs go off shortly after I made my commitment to the Lord. A student named Bill was the first person at Biola to disciple me. He was an ex-Marine in his mid-twenties who seemed totally dedicated to God. I admired him tremendously. We handed out Christian tracts on the corner of Hollywood and Vine and visited jail inmates together. Whenever I went by Bill's dorm room, I'd find him on his bed, reading the Bible.

To my surprise, however, Bill left Biola in the middle of that first academic year. He got involved in a cult, began a relationship with a married woman, and abandoned the faith. I couldn't believe it. I wondered, *If Bill can't make it, how am I going to do it?*

Over the years, I've seen many more of these bombs go off. Rick and Cindi, for example, were a husband-and-wife team I knew that were heavily involved in missions work. Both were dedicated to their faith, two hard-working servants of the Lord. They and their two children moved to Wyoming to take over a church there. All seemed well at first, but then I heard an unbelievable report: Cindi had fallen for the youth pastor at the church. Her marriage to Rick was shattered.

Then there is Jerry, the man who preached my ordination service at a small church in Carver, Oregon. His son, Will, became my best friend at Biola, and Will and his parents practically adopted me during my school years. Jerry, his wife, Emily, and Will were a loving family, so different from my own. They were a wonderful blessing to me in those years.

While I was at Biola, Emily discovered she had leukemia. She passed away while I was at seminary. It was a sad time for me and a tremendous loss for Jerry and his family. A few years later, though, he recovered from his grief and married Charlene, an administrator at a Christian school. But almost immediately after the wedding, Jerry was shocked to discover that his new wife had been involved in a lesbian relationship. Equally devastating, he learned that Charlene had seduced girls at the Christian school, and that others in the administration knew and did nothing about it. Distressed and disillusioned, Jerry didn't just annul his marriage. He became very angry with God and for a time walked away from Him.

The stories go on and on.

I'm sure you can think of your own examples of people who completely lost their bearings. You may be one yourself. What happened to them? To you? How can men and women who put their trust in Christ make such terrible mistakes and turn away from Him and His ways? Why the seemingly sudden disconnect?

The answer can be found in Scripture. Solomon wrote, "The hearts of men, moreover, are full of evil and there is madness in their hearts while they live" (Ecclesiastes 9:3).

Jesus put it in even more graphic language:

"It's what comes out of a person that pollutes: obscenities, lusts, thefts, murders, adulteries, greed, depravity, deceptive dealings, carousing, mean looks, slander, arrogance, foolishness—all these are vomit from the heart. *There* is the source of your pollution" (Mark 7:21–23 MSG).

A Seed for Malice

Don't miss this biblical message: The heart is evil. Nearly every sin imaginable is "vomit from the heart." The heart is the source of the pollution in our lives.

You may be thinking, *What is this guy talking about? I may not be perfect, but my heart isn't evil. And my sweet little baby daughter certainly doesn't have all that "pollution" in her heart!*

Let's consider this for a moment. Why do we, as parents, work so hard to teach our kids to have good manners, to tell the truth, to treat others with kindness? When parents fail to address these issues, how do their children act? Isn't it true that without proper teaching and guidance, kids will descend into all manner of selfish and destructive behaviors? I'm sure you've seen it happen. It's just part of their nature—or stated more accurately, the condition of their hearts.

I'm not saying that we are born with a fully developed inclination toward evil, or that little children intend to harm and destroy with every thought and act (though I've occasionally met a mischievous boy or girl who made me wonder!). But I am stating that the *seed* for malice is there from the beginning. It's called sin, and it's what the apostle Paul was talking about when he wrote, "For before the law was given, sin was in the world" (Romans 5:13).

As children and then as adults, we carry around that sinful seed inside our hearts. The training of our parents—and for many of us, faith in Christ—helps us keep it buried. But then, so often, something happens that causes the seed to grow.

It can be anything: the death of a loved one, a life-threatening disease, a spouse's affair, an abortion, the loss of a job, emotional or sexual abuse, lies that destroy our reputation, bankruptcy.

The outcome is pain, a wound that penetrates to the core of our soul—to our hearts. And if we're not careful, the hurt becomes a trigger. The wound is like water on our buried sin. As the water flows, the sin grows and flourishes with each passing day.

All of us enter salvation with wounded hearts, some to a greater degree than others. Contrary to what we tend to believe, the Christian life does not automatically remove the hurt. Christ is not a Great Eraser who instantly wipes away the pain of your past. As a result, what often happens is that once we give our lives to Jesus and discover that we still have pain, we choose to self-medicate. We do whatever it takes to get by. And we wonder why God doesn't seem to care.

Dr. David Allen, a Christian psychologist and author, has described the process this way:

> The cycle is predictable. It goes like this: Internal pain (a void, sense of inadequacy, love hunger, or loss) manifests itself as shame, anxiety, guilt, depression, anger, or boredom. The vulnerable person tries to alleviate this pain or get comfort through some type of anesthetic—drugs, alcohol, relationships, work, rage, sex, food, or gambling. The anesthetic relieves the situation temporarily but later generates even more serious consequences—intense guilt, remorse, and dissatisfaction with self…God-given meaning, dignity, identity, and value for oneself are lost.[1]

Sound familiar? You probably know someone in your family, neighborhood, workplace, or church that's trapped in this cycle. You might be there yourself. Look again at the result: "God-given meaning, dignity, identity, and value for oneself are lost." It's a pattern that leads to crisis and tragedy. It's a spiral into despair. It's the definition of a wounded and troubled heart.

It's also the road I was on for most of my life—only I didn't know it.

HUMAN DOINGS

You could say that my childhood was less than ideal. Pornographic materials of various types were readily available in our home. My father had a serious drinking problem and a violent temper. He worked at menial jobs in the Oakland area and had no interests or hobbies other than working, drinking, and gambling. My mother was a hyperactive woman who worked at drug stores and led an active social life. I felt neglected and never bonded with her.

Conflict was commonplace in our family. My parents fought often and separated many times while I grew up. My older brother, Ron, and I couldn't stand each other and also fought. Once I threw him through the kitchen window. Another time, when I had my hands and feet tied as part of a game we were playing, he pushed me off the front porch and bloodied my face. The only person at home I didn't battle with was my brother Terry, ten years younger. We mostly left each other alone.

On top of all this, I was sexually abused multiple times by someone I trusted. For a child not even twelve years old, it was an overwhelming and frightening experience. I felt betrayed. I didn't know where to turn. It also awakened sexual feelings I wasn't ready for.

As you might expect, by the time I graduated from high school, I had hardened my heart and was stubborn, unfeeling, unloving, rebellious, negative, unhappy, and unfulfilled. I wouldn't have said so at the time, but I had a wounded and troubled heart.

Yet by the time I graduated from Biola and married Joan, I believed everything had changed. I was motivated to ride the fast track to bringing glory to God. The years passed like a runaway train. We moved to Portland, where I completed my seminary training at Western Conservative Baptist Seminary and served as part-time pastor of a community church. We spent nearly four years as missionaries in Brazil. Joan and I had two children. Then we felt the Lord leading us to start a new church in Corvallis, Oregon.

Those days at what became Northwest Hills Church were exciting and challenging. I wanted to be involved in everything. We had three morning services and an evening service. In addition to preparing several messages each week, I attended numerous weekly meetings. I also served as a board member and then chairman of the board of a missionary organization, became involved with other Christian organizations, and accepted out-of-town speaking engagements.

After fourteen years of full-time (and then some) ministry at Northwest Hills, we left for another ministry opportunity in Illinois, only to return to Corvallis several months later after discovering the position in Illinois wasn't what we anticipated. A group of close friends felt prompted to begin a new church. Despite the concerns of some people I'd served with for years, I agreed to help with this new effort.

Following a few years of working to establish this new church in Corvallis, Joan and I, along with our daughter, Jennifer, again left Corvallis for a year of missions work in Brazil (our eldest child, Tim, stayed behind to attend college). After Brazil came a short-term assignment with Medical Ambassadors International, seven years as pastor of Modesto (California) Covenant Church, a stint as pastor of Cascade Community Church in Sisters, Oregon, and a merger with Sisters Baptist Church. In Sisters, I was especially excited and proud when our son, Tim, was invited to join us as assistant pastor. I felt even more so a couple of years later when Tim agreed to become lead pastor, while I continued to serve as an associate pastor and also launched a new, international effort, World Leadership Ministries.

I should have been able to look back on my forty-plus years of ministry with satisfaction. I'd experienced amazing opportunities to serve God and had been blessed in countless ways. And yet…I wasn't happy. Though I'd refused to admit it to myself, through all those years I'd lived with a nagging sense of internal conflict. I often felt frustrated, guilty, and disillusioned. It was more than the usual bumps that go with trying to lead a family and congregation. I was so driven to perform for God that I missed out on the joy of life. Something at the core of my soul wasn't right.

But I didn't want to face that. My solution was to serve and then serve some more. I was a man in perpetual motion.

Dr. Allen has put into words the state of my life at that time:

Hurt people sometimes feel restless without knowing why; they find it hard to just be. They always have to be on the go—accomplishing something to help them feel good about themselves and escape the empty feelings quiet brings. They tend to be human doings rather than human beings.[2]

Year after year, the output of my life far exceeded the intake. I neglected my health, my family, and most importantly, my walk with God. Though my intentions were good, and though everything appeared under control from the outside, on the inside my heart became more troubled by the day. I could identify with the struggle the apostle Paul experienced and vividly describes in Romans 7:15: "I do not understand what I do. For what I want to do I do not do, but what I hate I do." I felt like a walking civil war.

Gradually the inner conflict, which at the time I was unable to identify as a severely wounded and troubled heart, intensified and grew to unbearable proportions. To ease the pain and tension, I made a series of sinful choices over the years, which included sexual failure, with more than one affair. What I did was sin. I now realize that because I had never let Jesus heal my troubled heart, the hidden chambers of my heart were unchanged. I was the perfect candidate for the time bomb inside me to explode.

Those terrible sins didn't make things better, of course. They made them far worse. I was racked by raging guilt and more internal conflict. I didn't want anyone to find out what I'd done. The incongruity between what I was preaching and teaching and what was going on in my personal life was tearing me apart. Yet I pressed on. Pride, fear, and the belief that I could solve my own problems all played a part in perpetuating my self-deception. My heart was more deeply troubled than ever, and I did nothing about it.

ARE YOU SO DULL?

But God has His ways. He loves us too much to allow us to continue to go down destructive paths indefinitely. I remember well the day several years ago when my world finally collapsed and God got my full attention.

It was a Monday morning. I was home alone when I noticed my son pull up in his jeep. When I opened the door and saw the look on Tim's face, I knew this was more than a social call.

> *God loves us too much to allow us to continue to go down destructive paths indefinitely.*

We sat in my living room, Tim on an easy chair and me on the couch. He quickly got to the point. He confronted me with an accusation he had heard about my sexual misconduct.

After a time of emotional discussion, Tim continued. His expression was serious and intense. "Dad, don't lie to me," he said. "If you do, you'll severely damage our relationship. But if this did happen and you tell the truth, you'll see grace like you've never seen before."

It was an excruciating moment. I was being confronted with my sins. I stayed calm on the outside, but my insides were churning.

"I've got to go upstairs," I said. I walked away.

Alone in my office, I was battered by a whirlwind of thoughts. The accusation *was* true. But if I admitted it, everything would change. So many people would be hurt. My reputation and maybe my marriage would be destroyed. Could I handle that?

On the other hand, could I continue with this charade of pretending to be someone I wasn't? Maybe this was God's way of grabbing me by the collar and putting an end to all these years of misery. After several minutes of intense struggle, God made it clear to me that now was the time to focus my full energies on finding some answers.

I dropped my head. *Yeah,* I thought. *It's time.*

I slowly walked downstairs and, with tears in my eyes, said, "It's true."

It was the beginning of the most tumultuous period of my life. The condition of my sinful heart was exposed and I knew as never before that I had a choice to make. I could continue to deny and rationalize my sin or face it head on and by God's grace find an answer to the disconnect I had been experiencing. I was overwhelmed by shame and guilt. I didn't think I could deal with the consequences of what I'd done. I began to rationalize that it might be better for Joan and the rest of our family and friends if I just disappeared. I fantasized about how I would make my escape and start a new life, maybe in Australia or New Zealand.

Yet in the end, I couldn't walk away from the people I loved and who loved me, or from what I knew was God's plan for restoring me. When I shared my struggle and confessed my sin to Joan, she made the choice to stand by me and work through this. We entered into the most intense and painful time we had experienced in our forty-plus years of marriage. But I was determined to do whatever it took to deal with the issues of my troubled heart that I had neglected far too long.

My quest for answers and the exposing of my sinful heart to the light started when Joan and I entered into a ten-day, intensive counseling session in Colorado. In some ways it was a very frustrating time. I wanted to talk about the specific mistakes I had made so I could figure out why I made them and how I could avoid them in the future. But the counselor kept insisting that just dealing with behaviors was like shuffling the chairs on the Titanic while it was going down. The issue wasn't my behaviors; it was the condition of my heart.

"Dennis," he said, "if your heart doesn't change, nothing will change." There it was again—it really was all about the heart. I couldn't get away from it!

After those ten days in Colorado, Joan and I said little to each other on the long drive back to Oregon. We were both disappointed. I felt we'd accomplished little during our time in counseling.

At home, though, I thought more deeply about the counselor's words and his focus on the heart. As I read my Bible, I started noticing how often the heart was mentioned. It was everywhere! I wondered if the counselor was on to something after all. I decided I needed to do my own study on matters of the heart in Scripture.

I still remember the summer evening I sat in my upstairs office, gazing out the window at our beautiful landscaped backyard, ponderosa pine trees framing our little pond and the waterfall that flows into it. The pastoral scene was such a contrast to my jagged thoughts and the mess I'd made of my life.

I opened my Bible and was soon reading Mark's Gospel. In chapter seven, Jesus tells a parable, but the disciples don't understand and ask Him about it.

"Are you so dull?" [Jesus] asked. "Don't you see that nothing that enters a man from the outside can make him 'unclean'? For it doesn't go into his heart but into his stomach, and then out of his body…What comes out of a man is what makes him 'unclean'…All these evils come from inside" (Mark 7:18–23).

Are you so dull? I stopped breathing for a moment. The words of Jesus seemed to echo off the walls of my office. He was trying to tell me something.

For most of my life, I realized, I'd thought the specific sinful choices I'd made were the cause of my trouble. If I could just learn to stop the sin, I figured, I'd be fine.

But maybe my approach was all wrong. Maybe the reason I was destroying my life with bad choices was that something was fundamentally wrong with my heart—and it had been there from the beginning. If I honestly wanted to get rid of the anguish that had been tormenting me for so many years, that's where I had to go. With the Lord's help, I had to confront the enemy inside me. I needed to embark on a journey to the center of my troubled heart.

Gordon MacDonald, in his helpful book *Rebuilding Your Broken World*, strongly emphasizes the need of dealing with the heart when he writes:

> A broken world will never be rebuilt until we learn this principle of the unbound heart. It must be unwrapped and exposed to the light. The light will show some unattractive evil, but then something wonderful will happen. The love of God will be free to flood into the dark recesses, and rebuilding will begin.[3]

Is this your story too? Do you live with a continual burden of frustration and confusion? Do you suffer from emotional pain that won't go away? Are you ruining your life and the lives of those around you with a stream of destructive acts?

It doesn't have to be this way. God doesn't want us to live this way. I've learned that He has so much more planned for me and for you. We can *know* His love and peace in a manner that is deep and satisfying—and never goes away.

It all starts with the heart.

A THOUGHT TO REMEMBER

Vulnerable people try to alleviate their pain through some type of self-medication.

A VERSE TO REVIEW

"O Sovereign Lord, deal well with me for your name's sake; out of the goodness of your love, deliver me. For I am poor and needy, and my heart is wounded within me."

PSALM 109:21–22

A QUESTION FOR REFLECTION

How has your heart been wounded?

CHAPTER TWO

EXPERIENCING A CHANGED HEART

*"To be human is to rebel. To be Christian is to supernaturally submit.
A Christian's heart is the battleground."*

GARY THOMAS

Look around, and I'll bet you'll soon come to the same conclusion I did: the heart matters. We use heart imagery to portray romantic love and talk about two hearts becoming one (where would Valentine's Day be without the heart?). We speak of happy people as lighthearted. We call courageous warriors "brave hearts." An intimate conversation is a "heart to heart." And if you're fully committed to someone, you love him or her "with all your heart."

The heart is just as important for describing the dark side of life. The loss of a lover leads to heartache and a broken heart. A cruel person is heartless. And when you lose your passion for something, your "heart isn't in it."

Yet as prominent as the heart is in our everyday world, it is even more important to our spiritual lives. In over a thousand references throughout the Bible, God makes it clear that the heart is His central concern. As Scripture says, "The LORD does not look at the things man looks at. Man looks at the outward appearance, but the LORD looks at the heart" (1 Samuel 16:7). What does God see when He looks at our hearts?

THE DIAGNOSIS

Ever had an electrocardiogram? A doctor places a series of electrodes on your body to measure electrical impulses generated by your heart. A machine produces a graph that shows how often, and how fast, your heart is beating. If you're in good shape, the chart reveals a series of evenly spaced jagged lines—none of the beats measuring too high or low, or too fast or slow. An EKG is a useful test for diagnosing all kinds of potential problems related to the heart.

Right now, though, I'd like you to take a different kind of test, one you might call a "spiritual EKG." You can use it to diagnose the health of your spiritual heart.

For this test, we're going to be looking for thirteen specific heart ailments listed by Jesus. The first seven are "inward" sinful attitudes that are harder to diagnose. The final six are "outward" sinful actions that may be visible to others who know you. All are deadly, however, and any one of them is the sign of a sinful heart.

Jesus describes them in Mark 7:21-22. "For from within, out of men's hearts, come *evil thoughts, sexual immorality, theft, murder, adultery, greed, malice, deceit, lewdness, envy, slander, arrogance and folly.*" Let's take a closer look at each one.

Sinful Attitudes (Inward)

1) EVIL THOUGHTS. Every outward act of sin is preceded by an inward sinful act of choice. It's amazing how our minds work.
2) GREED. "The accursed love of having." Are you never satisfied with what you have? Do you always want something bigger and better—a new computer, a new dress, a new house? Many of us struggle with an appetite that always wants more.
3) MALICE. A lingering desire to harm someone else—they got me, I want to get them.
4) DECEIT. Translated in Scripture from the Greek word for *bait*; crafty, cunning. Some people seem to lie and deceive even when they have no reason for it.
5) LEWDNESS. A disposition of soul that resents all discipline: no restraints, no sense of decency or shame.

6) ENVY. The "evil eye." It involves comparing yourself to others and want-
ing what they have—their success, their possessions, their happiness.

7) ARROGANCE. Literally "showing our self above." It means displaying a
degree of contempt for everyone except yourself. Once again, it involves
comparisons and thoughts such as *I would never do that* or *I can't understand that jerk!*

These are the inward sins that men may not observe, but God clearly sees.
Then there are sinful actions. We see them every day, in the newspaper and in
our own lives.

Sinful Actions (Outward)

1) SEXUAL IMMORALITY. The Greek word used in Scripture for this is
porneia, the root of the English word *pornography.* It means every kind
of traffic in sexual vice. In today's highly sexualized society, it is one of
the leading indicators of a troubled heart.

2) THEFT. Taking what doesn't belong to you. It could mean using the
handicapped parking spot at the grocery store, embezzling funds from
your employer, and anything in between.

3) MURDER. The taking of an innocent life.

4) ADULTERY. Sexual involvement with anyone other than one's spouse. It
was a problem for King David in Old Testament times. It's still a problem today.

5) SLANDER. Insulting man or God. Though this may seem a specialty of
politicians during campaign season, we all must be on our guard for
this one.

6) FOLLY. Moral folly; playing the fool. Ever act without thinking on a foolish, selfish impulse? That's trouble!

These are the thirteen ailments that Christ has described as "vomit from
the heart." Not a pretty list, is it? This list is not exhaustive but is indicative
of what lurks in the human heart. But let's be honest—we've all had
moments of struggle with a few of these, and perhaps many of them. The

question is, what are you going to do about it?

I suggest you start with a self-examination—an EKG of your spiritual heart. Go back to the list above and write down each sinful action or attitude on a piece of paper. Then stop for a minute at each one, review your behavior, and ask yourself: Is this a recurring problem in my life? I'm not talking about if you once had a mean thought when a driver cut in front of you in traffic. Is this part of your everyday routine, something you struggle with on a regular basis? Write down the answer on your paper. Don't try to pass over any ugly truths—your honesty now is one of the keys to unlocking your future.

Now that you're finished, what's the diagnosis? The prognosis may not look good. The doctors may even be calling for life support. And you're lying on the table, asking, "How did this happen?"

Believe me, it's a common story—one as old as mankind.

The Devastated Heart

When God created the first man and woman, He made humans, not machines. God gave Adam and Eve rational and moral natures, so it was necessary that they be tested. When the Lord put Adam and Eve in the garden, He said, "You are free to eat from any tree in the garden; but you must not eat from the tree of the knowledge of good and evil" (Genesis 2:16–17). The test God gave forbade the minimum and allowed the maximum. But you know what happened and it's the same path we still go down when confronted with temptation. Satan isn't very creative. He doesn't have to be. His old pattern still works.

When we look at the third chapter of Genesis, we see five downward steps that we know all too well:

1) LISTENING: "[The serpent] said to the woman, 'Did God really say, "You must not eat from any tree in the garden"?'" (v. 1).

    Satan speaks to us with deviant messages placed throughout our culture and even in our own minds. The messages are like TV commercials. You know it's best to tune them out, but sometimes, like Eve, you stop and listen—just for a minute.

2) LOOSENING: "But God did say, 'You must not eat from the tree that is in the middle of the garden, and you must not touch it'" (v. 3).

Satan can be subtle, and even a subtle change can have dangerous consequences. The serpent asked Eve whether God really said she couldn't eat from any tree. Eve corrected him, saying God's only restriction was eating from the tree of the knowledge of good and evil. But then she attributed a new statement to God, that "you must not touch it." Eve added to the Word of God. She loosened her hold on what the Lord had actually said.

Once you loosen your hold on the Word of God by adding to it or subtracting from it and think He doesn't really mean what He says—or say, "Yes, that's true for you, but not necessarily true for me"—then it's like letting go of your anchor at sea. You're setting yourself adrift and headed for a storm.

3) LOOKING: "The woman saw the fruit of the tree was good" (v. 6).

When Eve looked, she decided that the fruit looked pretty good! *Why, she thought, would a good God withhold anything like this from me?* It starts with the eyes and launches a thought progression that leads to trouble.

4) LONGING: "[The fruit] was pleasing to the eye, and also desirable for gaining wisdom" (v. 6).

The longer Eve looked at the fruit, the stronger her longing for it grew. Satan has ways to make any sin appear desirable. The more our eyes dwell in places they shouldn't, the easier it is to cross the line.

5) LAYING HOLD OF: "She took some and ate it" (v. 6).

Eve pulled the fruit off the tree, ate it, and as the saying goes, the rest is history. All the problems you or I have in life, all the problems our world has, can be traced right back to these five steps Adam and Eve took in the Garden of Eden.

Ravi Zacharias says, "Evil is not just where blood has been spilled. Evil is in the self-absorbed human heart."[1] That's where it starts. Sin is basically man's rebellion against the authority of God and pride in his own supposed self-adequacy. This results in alienation from God.

We are left with a desperate need to have our hearts radically changed by Christ.

CONVERSION

When we commit our lives to Jesus, what is really happening? Our hearts are being transformed. From the inside out, we begin activating the faith we were meant to experience. This spiritual conversion takes place in three dimensions of our hearts: our intellect, our emotions, and our will.

For many people, conversion begins with the intellect. There is a fact-based, positive recognition of the truth of the Bible and the person of Christ. There is at least some understanding of the facts of who Jesus is and what He did. Many people in our culture have had an intellectual conversion. Every Sunday, churches across the country are filled with people who have investigated, thought it through, and believe the propositional truth. You don't put your brains on the shelf when you become a Christian.

Conversion takes place when we invite the Living Christ to change our hearts.

But don't stop there—nobody goes into heaven head first!

The second dimension of the heart is emotional. That's where the Holy Spirit enables a passionate drawing of your heart to the truth and person of Christ. Jason, a man who attended one of the churches I pastored years ago, recalled that he knew *about* Christ, but it wasn't until a day in church when the words of Scripture seemed to physically reach out and grab him that he *felt* the presence of Jesus. At that moment, tears came to Jason's eyes. Something had happened to him. His emotions had finally caught up with his intellectual understanding.

The last dimension of the heart is volitional. It's a matter of the will—a decision. You may believe in God and sense His presence in a compelling way, yet still hold back from following Him. You must *choose* to commit your life to Christ. As the apostle Paul wrote, "If you confess with your mouth, 'Jesus is Lord,' and believe in your heart that God raised him from the dead, you will be saved" (Romans 10:9).

It's like the inner workings of a grandfather clock—every element must be in sync for that clock to keep running and keep accurate time. In the same way, you won't know true spiritual conversion until all three dimensions of the heart—intellect, emotions, and will—are working together.

I once had the privilege of watching these three dimensions come together in a strong and powerful way. Years ago, I served as board chair for a missions organization that was going through a crisis with its team in the Philippines. I was asked to travel there to help with the situation. I went to Dr. Robert Nichols to get my immunization shots for the trip. I'd met him only recently. His son-in-law had been killed in a car accident and I'd counseled the family. I knew that Robert was not a believer.

When Robert learned where I was going, he said he'd like to go too. As a joke, I said, "Well, why don't you come along?"

The next day, Robert called and asked if I was serious about my invitation to the Philippines. "No!" I said. "This isn't a pleasure trip. I'll be there just a few days and I'll be in meetings the whole time."

Robert said he really wanted to go. I explained that I was leaving soon; he wouldn't have time to arrange for tickets, a passport, and a visa. Robert insisted that he could get the paperwork done on time.

"You don't understand," I said. "I'll be busy the entire time I'm there. I won't even have time to talk to you."

"That's all right," Robert said. "I can talk with you on the plane."

I didn't understand why Robert was so persistent. *Lord, what are You doing here?* I thought. *I hardly know this man.* But eventually I relented.

Three days later, Robert and I sat together on a Boeing 727 for the long flight to Manila. We talked the entire time, with Robert firing question after question at me. How do you know the Bible is really the Word of God? What about people who've never heard of Jesus? Is Christ really the only way to salvation? The tragic death of Robert's son-in-law had inspired a searching self-examination. I realized he was sincerely seeking the truth. He was trying to satisfy the intellectual dimension of his heart.

It wasn't until after we landed, however, that I discovered just how much was going on with Robert during our trip. A group from our missionary team picked us up at the airport and took us out to eat. I hadn't had a chance to explain Robert's presence. I kept looking for a moment to pull them aside and let them know he wasn't a believer.

I never got the chance. Just after we sat down in the restaurant, one of the men with us looked at Robert and asked, "Doc, when did you come to know the Lord?"

I cringed, fearing an awkward moment for Robert and for me. I'll never forget his answer. Robert looked at his watch and said, "When? Oh, about six hours ago at thirty thousand feet."

Somewhere over the Pacific Ocean, Robert had invited the Lord into his heart. He'd experienced spiritual conversion. Robert was excited—he'd committed himself to the Lord, entered into a holy relationship, and was looking at a bright new future. He'd left the struggles and miseries of his old life behind.

Or had he?

Converted But Not Consecrated

When a person experiences spiritual conversion, he gains a new heart. God says, "I will give you a new heart and put a new spirit in you; I will remove from you your heart of stone and give you a heart of flesh" (Ezekiel 36:26). The Lord fills that new heart with love: "God has poured out his love into our hearts by the Holy Spirit, whom he has given us" (Romans 5:5).

The new believer is "born again" (1 Peter 1:23) and takes on a new identity: "For if a man is in Christ he becomes a new person altogether—the past is finished and gone, everything has become fresh and new" (2 Corinthians 5:17 Phillips).

The past is gone. Everything is fresh and new. It all sounds pretty good, right? And it is—it's the most wonderful thing that can happen to a man or woman on this side of heaven.

But there's one little piece that's missing from this picture—a key element that needs to fall into place. It's easy to understand, yet so very difficult to do. When we give our lives to the Lord, we must change our focus. Our purpose now is no longer to just take care of ourselves and our families. Instead, "we make it our goal to please him" (2 Corinthians 5:9). It's not about us now. It's about Him.

There's a word for this vital step in order to experience God's best: *consecration*. It means that we are devoting ourselves wholeheartedly to the Lord. As the Bible says, "Your hearts must be fully committed to the Lord our God, to live by his decrees and obey his commands" (1 Kings 8:61). According to M. H. Miller, "consecration is handing God a blank sheet to fill in with your name signed at the bottom."

Consecration means consenting to God's supremacy in all things. This is what Jesus had in mind when He said, "If anyone would come after me, he must deny himself and take up his cross daily and follow me" (Luke 9:23). There is a moment of consecration and then a process of consecration—an ongoing commitment to daily obedience. God is the boss. I want to do it His way. When I find myself doing things my way, I have to stop and pray, "Lord, not my will, but Yours."

Consecration is the process of changing from a self-centered life to a God-centered life. Let's face it—many of us are very self-centered. This is what *I* want. This is what works for *me*. Consecration is letting God work in us so that life is no longer about ourselves. We want to come to the place where we always desire to seek His kingdom first. That's when everything else starts working as it should.

Consecration is the process of changing from a self-centered life to a God-centered life.

So many Christians today are converted but not consecrated. If you accepted the Lord as a child, you were certainly welcomed into the family of God, but likely not consecrated. If you entered into salvation as an adult, you still probably lacked the spiritual maturity and biblical understanding to also be consecrated—to devote yourself without reservation to God's way.

What's the result of this converted, yet unconsecrated life? You can guess the answer: a troubled heart.

FREEING THE CHANGED HEART

Remember what we learned in the first chapter? Our hearts are "full of evil" and need to be changed. We may be converted. We may have salvation. We've undergone a spiritual change. We may even have consecrated our lives to the Lord. Yet in this life, we'll never know the deep joy that comes from joining God's family if our plan is simply to go to church and try to follow the rules. We'll battle daily with temptation and lose most of the time.

When Jesus listed His thirteen "heart ailments," He took the focus of attention away from external rituals and placed it on the need for God to change—to *renovate*—our sinful hearts. This process begins when we are genuinely converted and consecrate our lives to Him. However, we still may need to have our hearts freed from the chains that keep us in bondage so that we can experience all that God promises.

Is your heart still in bondage? Do you sense that something is holding you back from the joy and peace that the Lord offers even though you have received Christ as your Savior and desire to live for Him? You may be struggling from unresolved spiritual and emotional conflicts. As Dr. David Allen explains, there's still work that needs to be done in our hearts.

> Our challenge is to become missionaries to our own hearts. So often we forget the painful feelings buried deep inside us—anger, fear, guilt— and the experiences that led us to feel that way. The heart is the repository for those painful feelings, but like a sponge it can only absorb so much emotion. Once it's saturated, there's little room left for love and joy and beauty.[2]

My research and my own personal experience have shown that there are three major issues that prevent men and women from living with a free heart. They are:

- GUILT in our relationship with God. This is a *vertical* issue.
- BITTERNESS in our relationship with others. This is a *horizontal* issue.
- ANXIETY in our relationship with ourselves. This is an *internal* issue.

Hearts must be free from guilt, bitterness, and anxiety. If you are not free from all three, watch out—the timer has been set, and sooner or later you're going to implode or explode. The good news is that when you know where to look, Scripture gives clear guidance on how to deal with each of these core issues. You *can* unshackle your heart and experience a life of love and peace. You'll be able to say, like the psalmist, "I run in the path of your commands, for you have set my heart free" (Psalm 119:32).

Chances are, if you're reading this book, that at least one of these issues is plaguing you right now. Let's dig deeper and find out.

A THOUGHT TO REMEMBER

A Christian's heart is the battleground.

A VERSE TO REVIEW

"If you confess with your mouth, 'Jesus is Lord,' and believe in your heart that
God raised him from the dead, you will be saved.
For it is with your heart that you believe and are justified, and
it is with your mouth that you confess and are saved."

ROMANS 10:9–10

A QUESTION FOR REFLECTION

Have you received a new heart by accepting Christ as your Savior?

CHAPTER THREE

FREEING THE GUILTY HEART

VERTICAL: OUR RELATIONSHIP WITH GOD

*"I am convinced that the greatest single cause of spiritual defeat
is a guilty conscience."*

ERWIN LUTZER

Elaine sat alone in her living room, fingered the photograph in her hand, and tried to hold back the tears. The image showed a mother and her five-year-old daughter with their arms around each other, beaming for the camera. The mother was Elaine's niece. The five-year-old was the first granddaughter of Elaine's sister. Elaine could see the family resemblance in the little girl's smile. It reminded her of her sister, even a bit of Elaine herself.

I could have been a grandmother now, Elaine thought. *That could be my daughter and granddaughter smiling at the camera. On holidays, I could have had a houseful of children and grandchildren gathered around the dining room table, and my husband—*

Elaine couldn't hold back any longer. The tears flowed down her cheeks. She made no attempt to wipe them away. *If only…*

It had happened forty years ago. She'd been sixteen at the time and living in Ohio. When Elaine had learned she was pregnant, she didn't know what to do. She wasn't ready to be a mother. Her parents were so disappointed and ashamed. Elaine herself was overwhelmed, nearly distraught. An abortion seemed the only solution. She didn't tell her parents until after it was over, after that horrible visit to the clinic downtown.

From that point on, everything in Elaine's life changed. Her parents still insisted she marry the father. That union lasted only a few months; Elaine had it annulled. She graduated from high school and met an older, studious boy named Steve. He wanted to teach. They fell in love, married when Elaine was nineteen, and moved to the West Coast when Steve graduated from college.

Thirty-six years later, Steve was a professor of history at an Oregon university. They'd tried without success to have children. It was a deep and mostly unspoken disappointment for both of them. An even greater strain on their marriage was the guilt Elaine carried with her over the abortion. Night after night, the terrible conversation with her conscience continued. *What was I thinking? I killed my child. I threw away the only chance I'll ever have for a son or daughter. How could I have been so blind? What will I tell my precious boy or girl when we meet in heaven? How can I ever explain or justify what I've done?*

Elaine confessed her mistake repeatedly to God. She knew from her Bible that the Lord forgives and forgets. Yet she never allowed *herself* to forget.

Then came the day when Steve gently confronted her. Their relationship had no life to it, he'd said. They'd grown apart. He'd found someone else, a woman who worked at the university. The marriage was over. He was moving out.

For Elaine, Steve's departure simply added another layer of guilt. She believed her constant brooding over the years had poisoned their marriage. She had driven Steve into the arms of another woman. Elaine lost all hope of happiness. She was drowning in guilt. She rarely went out and hardly spoke to her friends. She didn't try to find a job. She no longer went to church. What was the point?

SEVEN TRAPS

For more than four decades, Elaine carried a heavy burden of guilt. It affected her marriage, her spiritual walk, and every other aspect of her life. She had confessed her sin and been forgiven of her sin by God, yet she was living in defeat.

You may be thinking, *It's not supposed to work like that*—and you're right. The Lord does not want us to live with guilt. It is one of the most painful emotions in human experience. It is a plague on our soul that poisons everything we think and do. Guilt is like a tiny weed that, if allowed to grow unchecked, can take over your heart and your life.

Pastor and bestselling author Rick Warren has written, "Many people are driven by guilt. They spend their entire lives running from regrets and hiding their shame. Guilt-driven people are manipulated by memories. They allow their past to control their future. They often unconsciously punish themselves by sabotaging their own success."[1]

Guilt is a plague on our soul that poisons everything we think and do.

Elaine was a person who continually punished herself. She allowed her past mistakes to limit her future. Her heart was trapped by guilt. How did it happen to her? How does the same thing happen to so many of us? Are you trapped by guilt right now?

I believe there are seven traps that most often ensnare us. Let's look at each of the seven.

1) CONFESSION IS NOT COMPLETE. One reason for guilt is a partial confession. We may have admitted to borrowing the car without permission, but neglected to mention the huge dent in the back fender. We feel guilty because we *are* guilty. We haven't owned our own stuff.

The Bible says, "He who conceals his sins does not prosper, but whoever confesses and renounces them finds mercy" (Proverbs 28:13). It also says, "But if we freely admit that we have sinned, we find him reliable and just—he forgives our sins and makes us thoroughly clean from all that is evil" (1 John 1:9 PHILLIPS).

An incomplete confession is a black stain on our hearts. God will wipe it clean only when we reveal our hearts and all of our sins. Excuses and rationalizations only prolong the pain.

2) REPENTANCE IS NOT GENUINE. It is possible to say the words and not mean any of them. When a husband tells his wife, "I'm sorry I gambled away our paycheck. I blew it. Please forgive me," and then does the same thing two weeks later, his repentance may not be real.

In the book of Jeremiah, God says, "Judah did not return to me with all her heart, but only in pretense" (Jeremiah 3:10). Confession without genuine repentance is meaningless. The apostle Paul wrote, "Godly sorrow brings repentance that leads to salvation and leaves no regret" (2 Corinthians 7:10). Repentance must include a heartfelt sorrow for sin and a decisive turning away from evil.

3) RESTITUTION IS LACKING. Maybe we have confessed our mistakes, owned and turned from our sin, and still there is guilt. If we have taken advantage of someone, we must go to them and make things right. In the Old Testament, we see that if a man steals livestock, he is expected to pay back four or five times what he took. If a man allows his livestock to graze in another man's field, restitution is expected. If a man starts a fire, he must pay for the damages (Exodus 22:1–6).

Guilt will continue to reside in our hearts until we settle with those we have harmed. As the theologian Augustine once said, "Without restitution, no remission."

4) SATAN IS ACCUSING. The devil does not want us to forget the terrible things we've done. He uses our mistakes to accuse us of being evil and undeserving of God's love. For forty years after her abortion, Elaine heard those accusations. Even when she made a conscious effort to put the abortion out of her mind, she was haunted by thoughts of unworthiness.

A man named Joe is one of my longtime friends. I was the best man at his wedding. But that marriage blew apart after twenty-plus years. The next one didn't last either. Joe blames himself for both divorces. He says he was harsh and insensitive with both wives, and that as a pastor, he put his ministry ahead of his family. He eventually gave up his ministry and grew distant from God. Recently, after Joe had restored his relationship with the Lord, I encouraged him to get back into the game. "I can't do it, Dennis," he said. "I've blown it and I can't forget it."

I believe both Elaine and Joe were under spiritual attack. Satan was doing his best to keep them trapped in the dark world of guilt. Scripture describes the devil as an accuser: "For the accuser of our brothers, who accuses them before our God day and night, has been hurled down" (Revelation 12:10). He uses accusations as a weapon to sustain our guilt.

5) OTHERS ARE UNFORGIVING. It isn't easy to move past the guilt when a spouse, friend, son, or daughter keeps bringing up your past mistakes. When a husband tells his wife, "I'll stay married to you, but I'll never forgive you for your

affair," the pain of guilt can feel like repeated stabs with a knife.

David once said, "I am in deep distress. Let us fall into the hands of the LORD, for his mercy is great; but do not let me fall into the hands of men" (2 Samuel 24:14). David understood that men and women have a desire for revenge. When someone is hurt, so often the response is to hurt back. Without forgiveness, it may continue day after day, year after year.

6) CIRCUMSTANCES KEEP REMINDING. When we're constantly faced with the result of our sin, it's harder to put it behind us. Elaine connected her abortion to the breakup of her marriage. For her, Steve's absence was a continuing reminder of her mistakes.

Sometimes the past can't be restored: "For I know my transgressions, and my sin is always before me" (Psalm 51:3). Divorce leads to an empty house. Careless driving leaves a family member confined to a wheelchair. Murder leads to a lifelong prison term. When circumstances continually confront us with our sin, guilt often follows.

7) WE ARE CONTINUALLY REHEARSING. We have a great ability to forget what we want to remember—where we left our car keys, the password to our Internet account—and to remember what we want to forget. Elaine could not seem to forget about her abortion. She had trained her mind to focus almost daily on what had happened, and nearly let it destroy her life. I have had similar struggles. It's so easy to rehash the past and beat ourselves up over what we've done.

David could easily have been thinking of Elaine or me when he wrote, "For I am about to fall, and my pain is ever with me. I confess my iniquity, I am troubled by my sin" (Psalm 38:17–18).

If we repeat thoughts and internal accusations such as *What a jerk I am, How stupid of me, I blew it,* and *I'm no good* often enough, we'll eventually believe them. That's not where God wants us to go.

I urge you to carefully consider right now the causes of guilt we've just discussed. Is Satan using any of these to keep you from God's peace? Are you feeling guilty without even realizing it? Have you, like Elaine, needlessly endured years of suffering for a sin that's already been forgotten by God?

It's not supposed to work like that. The Lord has another plan.

POWERFUL RESOLUTIONS

Let's say that you *have* identified a mistake—a sin—that continues to bring guilt into your life. Maybe, like Elaine, it was an abortion. Maybe you blew your family's savings account on a drunken binge. Or you invented a lie that ruined a reputation. Or you stole from your employer. Or the last time you saw your father, you had a vicious argument that ended with hurtful words.

Whatever it is, you *can* free your heart of this burden. The place to start is to ask yourself these questions and answer each one honestly:

Have I confessed all of my sin to God?
Have I asked for His forgiveness?
Is my repentance genuine?
Have I gone to everyone my sin has harmed and tried to make things right?

If the answer to any of these questions is "No," then you have work to do! You cannot expect to break free of guilt unless you are willing to make the effort to throw off the shackles. God will guide you on the correct path, but you must take the steps. Don't put it off—your happiness depends on dealing with this issue today.

I tell people who have completely confessed their sin to the Lord, genuinely repented, and made restitution that they should never confess that sin again. God does not reintroduce forgiven sin. Repeated confessions are proof that we are relying on our feelings instead of our faith. We must take God at His Word— we are free to forget what He has freely and fully forgiven.

W. M. Czamanske once wrote, "In response to the question, 'Do you feel that you have been forgiven?' Martin Luther answered, 'No, but I'm as sure as there's a God in heaven. For feelings come and feelings go, and feelings are deceiving; my warranty is the Word of God—nothing else is worth believing. Though all my heart should feel condemned for want of some sweet token, there is One greater than my heart whose Word cannot be broken. I'll trust in God's unchanging Word till soul and body sever; for though all things shall pass away, His Word shall stand forever!'"

As you move through these powerful resolutions to feelings of guilt, keep in mind three spiritual truths. They will give you the confidence you need as you speak with God and those you have hurt. They will help you drop your burden of guilt on the side of the road and leave it there as you journey into the future He has planned for you.

1) ALL MY SINS ARE OUT OF GOD'S SIGHT. When King Hezekiah offered a prayer of gratitude to the Lord for restoring his health, he said, "You have put all my sins behind your back" (Isaiah 38:17). This is what theologians call an anthropomorphic statement—using human terms to describe something that is hard to grasp. If something is behind your back, you don't see it. All of our forgiven sins are behind His back.

Put another way, God has "swept away your sins like the morning mists. I have scattered your offenses like the clouds" (Isaiah 44:22 NLT). The Lord takes the deepest, darkest stain and totally and permanently removes it. All of our forgiven sins are removed from His sight.

2) ALL MY SINS ARE OUT OF GOD'S REACH. Just how far away are our forgiven sins? According to David, "As far as the east is from the west, so far has he removed our transgressions from us" (Psalm 103:12). The most powerful telescope cannot bring our sins into focus.

Jerry Bridges, in his book *Transforming Grace,* explains further: "If you start due north at any point on earth, you would eventually cross over the North Pole and start going south, but that is not true when you go east or west. If you start west and continue in that direction, you will always be going west. North and south meet at the North Pole, but east and west never meet. In a sense, they are an infinite distance apart. So when God says He removes our transgressions from us as far as the east is from the west, He is saying they have been removed an infinite distance from us. But how can we get a 'handle' on this rather abstract truth in such a way that it becomes meaningful in our lives?

"When God uses this expression to describe the extent of His forgiveness, He is saying His forgiveness is total, complete, and unconditional. He is saying He is not keeping score with regard to our sins...How can God possibly do this? The answer is by His grace through Jesus Christ."[2]

3) ALL MY SINS ARE OUT OF GOD'S MIND. What God forgives, He forgets: "For I will forgive their wickedness and will remember their sins no more" (Jeremiah 31:34). When we bring to the Lord sins that have been confessed and forgiven, He says to us, "If you want to remember what I forgot, that is your

privilege. But I would suggest you learn to forget what I have forgotten!"

It takes a mature faith to accept God's forgiveness and forgive ourselves. David Allen describes it this way: "Mature spirituality requires the dethronement of guilt and bitter feelings as we recognize the total forgiveness provided through God's love. That means emptying our negative feelings daily at the cross and allowing the grace of God to fill the gap between the real and ideal levels of our life."[3]

Trading guilt for grace is a daily process. You may find it difficult, especially at first. The more you nourish your faith, the easier it will be.

Purposeful Responses

A boy named Johnny was staying with his grandparents on their farm. They gave him a slingshot to play with. He practiced with a target in the woods but could never seem to hit it. One day, after a particularly discouraging day in the woods, he headed back to the farmhouse for dinner. On the way he spied his grandmother's pet duck. On impulse, Johnny armed his slingshot, aimed at the duck, and let fly. To Johnny's amazement, the rock hit the duck square on the head, killing it.

Johnny couldn't believe it. In a panic, he hid the duck in a pile of wood. When he turned around, there stood his sister, Sally. She had seen it all but said nothing.

After the children's lunch the next day, their grandmother said, "Sally, let's wash the dishes."

Sally said, "Grandma, Johnny told me he wanted to help in the kitchen." She whispered to Johnny, "Remember the duck?" So Johnny did the dishes.

Later that day, Grandpa asked if the children wanted to go fishing. Grandma said, "I'm sorry, but Sally will have to stay. I need her help to make supper."

Sally smiled. "Maybe I can go, because Johnny told me he wanted to help with supper." Johnny again heard his sister's whisper: "Remember the duck?" So Sally went fishing and Johnny stayed behind to help.

For the next several days, Johnny did his own chores and Sally's. Finally, he couldn't stand it any longer. He walked up to his grandmother and with tears in his eyes confessed that he had killed the duck.

His grandmother knelt down, gave Johnny a hug, and said, "Sweetheart, I know. You see, I was standing at the window and I saw the whole thing. But because I love you, I forgave you. I was just wondering how long you would let Sally make a slave of you."

Sooner or later, we all mess up. We make mistakes that offend God and hurt others. The devil will use those mistakes to make us his slaves.

The question becomes, how do we respond to our mistakes? Do we hang onto our guilt and allow the devil to use it against us? Or do we give our mistakes and our guilt to God and ask Him to forgive us? Remember, the Lord already knows about it. He was standing at the window and saw the whole thing. He loves us and is ready to forgive us.

As you consider your response to your sin and feelings of guilt, I recommend you run through the following checklist. It may help you to put guilt in its place.

- ✓ RECOGNIZE the author of recurring bad memories. Satan loves to bring up your past and destroy your future. As someone has said, "When Satan reminds you of your past, you remind him of his future!"
- ✓ RESIST the devil's accusations. Don't let him set the agenda. Keep turning to the Lord and eventually the enemy will quit hassling you: "Submit yourselves, then, to God. Resist the devil, and he will flee from you" (James 4:7).

    How did Jesus respond to the devil's temptations in the desert? He repeatedly turned to God's Word, the sword of the Spirit: "It is written..." (Matthew 4:4); "It is also written..." (Matthew 4:7); "Away from me, Satan! For it is written..." (Matthew 4:10). Memorize those statements and use them to fight back. Tell the enemy, "I won't go there!"
- ✓ REMEMBER that the cross is the only way to deal with your past. Jesus died for *all* our sins—past, present, and future. The cross and the empty tomb stand between us and the haunting memories of the past. Let Paul's words encourage you: "God made you alive with Christ. He forgave us all our sins, having canceled the written code, with its regulations, that was against us and that stood opposed to us; he took it away, nailing it to the cross. And having disarmed the powers and authorities, he made

a public spectacle of them, triumphing over them by the cross" (Colossians 2:13–15).

✓ REFUSE to punish yourself by remembering and rehearsing past sins. Say to yourself, "I won't do that!" Randy Alcorn has written, "Refusing to forgive ourselves is an act of pride—it's making ourselves and our sins bigger than God and His grace."[4] We cannot see the way forward in our journey as Christians if we are constantly looking in the rearview mirror of our past mistakes.

✓ REJOICE in God's complete forgiveness—sing to and praise Him. Turn your moans and groans about what you've done into words and songs of gratitude for God's love and mercy. Remember the words of David: "He lifted me out of the pit of despair, out of the mud and the mire. He set my feet on solid ground and steadied me as I walked along. He has given me a new song to sing, a hymn of praise to our God" (Psalm 40:2–3 NLT).

Commit to working through these responses to guilt feelings and you will be on your way to freedom. Leave thoughts of *if only* and *I should have* behind. You don't have to "sell" God on your sincerity. He already knows your heart. He wants to renew it with His grace.

A GUILT-FREE LIFE

Remember Elaine, the woman who had the abortion? She came to see me not long after the divorce from her husband, Stephen. I could see immediately how distressed she was. As she explained her story, I understood just how long and how deep her entrapment went. She had been a slave to guilt for most of her life.

No sin is too great for God to pardon.

As we talked, I explained to Elaine that through God's grace, no sin is too great for Him to pardon, that His forgiveness extends as far as east is from west. We talked about how the Lord wanted her to take a stand against Satan and regain control of her thoughts.

The more we discussed these things, the more I began to observe flickers of hope in Elaine's eyes. I could see relief, even a hint of joy. Her journey out of the trap of guilt was only just beginning, but for the first time in perhaps many years, Elaine was picturing the guilt-free path God wanted for her life.

He wants that same path for you too. He desires to have a relationship with you that is unobstructed by guilt. He wants your heart to be free. If guilt is holding you back, I urge you to read this chapter again and put these principles into practice. I can guarantee that they work, because they don't come from me—they come from the Lord. They are your keys to a guilt-free life.

And if you've determined that guilt isn't your problem…please keep reading.

A THOUGHT TO REMEMBER

The cross and the empty tomb stand between us and
the haunting memories of the past.

A VERSE TO REVIEW

"As far as the east is from the west, so far
has he removed our transgressions from us."

PSALM 103:12

A QUESTION FOR REFLECTION

Do you really believe God has fully forgiven and forgotten all of your sins?

CHAPTER FOUR

FREEING THE BITTER HEART

HORIZONTAL: OUR RELATIONSHIP WITH OTHERS

Bitterness is like "battery acid in the soul."

NEIL T. ANDERSON

I still can't believe it. I hate 'em both. I hate 'em!"

The voice belonged to an overweight man sitting at a round kitchen table. He held a cup of coffee in one hand and a cigarette in the other, and waved both as he spoke. A woman sat across from him at the table with another cup of coffee and nodded in agreement. I stood in front of the sink, poured myself a glass of water, and tried to stay out of the line of fire.

"He's a crook, that's what he is," the man said. "If he'd given us half what we deserved, things would be different around here."

The woman nodded again. "Mom's just as much to blame," she said. "He was always her favorite. We were the black sheep."

The man at the table was my Uncle Bob, and the woman with him was my mother. I was on a break from college classes and staying at my parents' home in Oakland, but my "vacation" was quickly turning sour. I knew what was coming as soon as Uncle Bob arrived for a visit. My grandmother had recently passed away. Before she died, my other uncle, Eldon, had persuaded her to sign over all her possessions to him. Eldon was executor of her estate. He'd sold everything— the house, the furniture, the cars, the rental properties, even the organ Grandma had wanted to leave to my wife. It was all gone, along with the money from the sales. So was Eldon—he'd disappeared.

I didn't blame Bob or my mother for being angry. I had been angry too. But I knew I had to let it go. Now, my uncle and mother were rehashing it all again, as they did every time they got together. I'd heard it so many times I knew the lines by heart.

"My own brother. How could he do it?" my uncle said. "What did I do to him to deserve this?"

I thought about Bob, a guy who'd been a practical joker all his life. Lately, the jokes had been less frequent, often replaced by angry outbursts. I watched his face as he talked. It was red and taut, the jaw set. The decibels of the words flying back and forth across the kitchen table increased and the gestures grew more animated. Suddenly, my uncle pounded the table so hard that the silverware jumped.

"I wish I knew where he was," he said. "I'd like to get my hands on him just once. He's ruined my life. I just want a few minutes to ruin his too."

The glass of water in my hand wasn't enough to clear my system of the poison that seemed to fill the room. I couldn't take it anymore. I left the house and went for a walk.

THE ROAD TO BITTERNESS

Bitterness. It is the most common and contagious hurtful condition that plagues our hearts. It is the easiest to justify. It is also the most difficult to diagnose. Most of us know when we feel guilty, but few of us are aware we are bitter. We may say we are hurt. We may talk about being disappointed. But bitter? We don't want to admit it—not to others, not to God, not even to ourselves.

Bitterness is like acid. It seeps into our lives before we're aware of it, corrodes our thoughts and our relationships, and if left unchecked burns a hole that reaches to our souls. It carries a cost none of us wants to pay.

So often, we don't see bitterness coming. One reason is that the road to a bitter heart takes time. It develops gradually. For most of us, it is a hidden process. It starts with an offense. You've heard the phrase, "bad things happen to good people." Sooner or later, one or more of those bad things happens to you. A friend betrays you. A loved one is suddenly taken away. A spouse abuses you emotionally. Rape. Divorce. Cancer. The list of potential offenses goes on. In this life, we all face moments where the unkind, unjust, or undeserved happens to us.

The next step on the road to bitterness is feeling hurt. We are wounded in our hearts. We feel pain that may debilitate us. We look for a way to deal with that pain. The answer, too often, is the third step: self-pity. We ask ourselves, *Why me? Why this? Why now?* Like my Uncle Bob, we say, "What did I do to deserve this?" We continually rehearse the damage done to us in an attempt to justify our desire to blame the offender.

If we linger in self-pity long enough, it leads us to the fourth step on the road to bitterness: anger. We seethe. Our blood pressure goes up. We think, *How could she do that to me?* or *If he wants to play hardball with me, I'll play hardball with him.* We want to lash out at the offender, and often do. At other times our anger spills over onto just about everyone else. People begin avoiding us because they don't want to be around an angry person.

If we don't deal with our anger, we reach the final destination on our journey: bitterness and resentment. We become prisoners of our own making. We are angry, discouraged, depressed, disillusioned, and unable to concentrate on our responsibilities or enjoy the relationships God has given us. We live with a sickness that steadily spreads to every corner of our lives. As David Seamands has written, "We cannot long ingest and integrate hidden resentment any more than our stomachs can digest and incorporate bits of broken glass."[1]

Bitterness robs us of vitality and joy. It gives Satan a foothold and hinders the work of the Spirit in our lives and churches.

Bitterness robs us of vitality and joy.

Do you recognize any of these symptoms in your life? Are you struggling with your relationships with your family, friends, and coworkers and don't know why? Is there an offense or tragedy, perhaps from long ago, that eats at your heart and soul? Have you unknowingly traveled the bumpy road to bitterness?

I encourage you to put this book down right now and think about your life. Take an honest look at the hard moments and how you responded to them. Do you feel any twinges of regret or resentment? Is there a corner of your heart that harbors bitter feelings? If so, you're not alone. Let's talk about how to leave bitterness behind and begin living the abundant life God has planned for you.

The Ultimate Pain Reliever

Perhaps after years of anguish, you're finally ready to admit it—you're living in pain and causing pain to others. You're filled with poison and want it out of your system. You have a firm grip on bitterness but you want to let it go. What now?

There is only one answer to your trouble. The prescription isn't easy, but it is the only remedy guaranteed to cure. It's the ultimate pain reliever. The path to freedom from bitterness is forgiveness from the heart.

"Oh, no," you say, shaking your head. "I'm not going to forgive after what he/she did to me. I'm not letting that person off the hook."

Before you throw this book in the trash, think for a moment about these next few words. Someone once said that "Unforgiveness is like drinking poison and then waiting for the other person to die." Do you understand that statement? You may refuse to forgive because you want to punish your offender. Yet the person who suffers the most is you. Your bitterness hurts your health and infects all of your relationships. Holding onto bitterness allows the offender to continue to traumatize you. Only forgiveness brings freedom.

David Allen describes what bitterness does to our hearts:

Whatever the causes of our injuries, if we do not work through them, the hurt begins to harden our hearts. The hardness contaminates us. We are less able to feel and touch and make connection with others. In other words, the resentment and hurt in our heart produces alienation within ourselves and also alienation from those around us. Lack of forgiveness destroys relationships, increases the isolation and fragmentation in our world…forgiveness is essential to the healing of the heart.[2]

To forgive does not mean to forget. It does not excuse anyone for what they did to you. It doesn't say you're "fine" with what happened. It does say, however, that you are going to stop letting it damage your life. Dr. Archibald Hart, a Christian psychologist, has said, "Forgiveness means giving up your right to hate someone for hurting you." The sooner you get that hate out of your system, the better off you will be.

Need another reason to forgive? It's biblical. Our Lord asks us to forgive "not up to seven times, but seventy times seven" (Matthew 18:22 AMP). In fact, our ability to forgive others is tied to God's willingness to forgive us: "If you hold anything against anyone, forgive him, so that your Father in heaven may forgive you your sins" (Mark 11:25).

Jesus didn't deserve to die on the cross, yet He sought mercy for His tormentors even as He was being crucified: "Father, forgive them, for they do not know what they are doing" (Luke 23:34). Jesus understands what it means to be hurt, to suffer, to feel humiliated. If our Lord is willing to endure that, forgive us, and even die for us, can't we find it in our hearts to forgive those who have offended us?

To forgive, we must let go of our grip on bitterness and instead grab hold of God's love, forgiveness, and sovereignty. We must be convinced that God rules and overrules. He has a plan for each of our lives. We are the only ones who can mess up that plan.

> *To forgive, we must let go of our grip on bitterness and instead grab hold of God's love, forgiveness, and sovereignty.*

C. S. Lewis wrote, "To be a Christian means to forgive the inexcusable, because God has forgiven the inexcusable in you."[3] Let's explore exactly how forgiving the inexcusable works.

PROGRESSING TO FORGIVENESS

For most of us, if we're bitter, forgiveness doesn't just "happen." After all, if our hearts are filled with bitterness, we don't want to forgive! Just as there is a process in reaching a state of bitterness, so too there is a progression to letting go of bitterness and arriving at forgiveness.

A study of Scripture shows that we must do each of the following:

- ACKNOWLEDGE any feelings of bitterness.
- ASSUME responsibility for your own wrong attitudes and actions.

- Adjust your focus of concentration from the offender to God.
- Abandon your desire to get even or take revenge.
- Ask God to use you to bless the offender.
- Act in obedience to the Holy Spirit's prompting.

There is spiritual power and lasting relief in each of these steps. We'll examine them in more detail.

Acknowledge Bitter Feelings

I once had to deal with a series of shattering accusations. Among them was the charge, completely false, that I had accepted church funds I wasn't entitled to. I was devastated and deeply hurt. When I tried to resolve the situation with my accusers, I got nowhere. Though I didn't realize it at the time, my frustration and pain soon grew into bitterness.

My family and I spent several days over the Christmas holiday that year in the home of two dear friends. Ed, the husband and a fellow pastor, was a great encourager and listener. It wasn't long before I began relating my troubles. To Ed, I'm sure my bitterness was obvious.

One evening, Ed asked for my help in preparing his message for that Sunday. It "happened" to be on Romans 12:9–21. We explored statements such as "Bless those who persecute you; bless and do not curse" (v. 14); "Live in harmony with one another" (v. 16); and "Do not take revenge, my friends, but leave room for God's wrath" (v. 19). Incredibly, I didn't see any connection between these verses and my bitter attitude. I simply wasn't ready to admit my bitterness.

After we finished, Ed showed me a sheepskin hanging on his upstairs railing. He said it reminded him that it was the Lamb of God, without spot or blemish, who shed His precious blood so we could be cleansed of all our sins. My friend then placed the sheepskin on the floor and gently asked me to kneel on it with him. From his knees, Ed petitioned God on my behalf. "Lord, thank You for the blood of Christ and for taking away our sins," he prayed. "Lamb of God, thank You for Dennis and for his life and ministry. Please release him now from the grip of all bitterness and sin."

When Ed finished, the Spirit of God moved upon me. Finally, I was ready to acknowledge the condition of my heart and release the garbage that had piled up inside of me. "Lord, I am a bitter man," I prayed. "I've been frustrated. I've been angry. I ask for Your forgiveness and Your grace. Please take away the bitterness."

Immediately, I felt a change. It was blessed relief. Joy and freedom flooded my soul.

In the Psalms, David wrote, "Trust in him at all times, O people; pour out your hearts to him, for God is our refuge" (Psalm 62:8). If we want to end the desperate spiral, we must acknowledge any feelings of bitterness to ourselves and then bring them before the Lord.

Assume Responsibility

Imagine that a neighbor borrows a few of your movie DVDs and music CDs and never returns them. You eventually confront her about it, and she has the gall to insist they belong to her! Not surprisingly, you develop a bitter attitude toward her and what's happened. You picture breaking into her home and stealing a few things yourself. You also let slip a few discourteous words about her to your friends.

Clearly, your neighbor is in the wrong. This is out-and-out theft. Compared to what she's done, your attitude and actions seem pretty minor. From your vantage point, she's 95 percent in the wrong and you're only in for about 5 percent. Makes sense, right?

The problem is that God doesn't want us to make comparisons or play percentages. He wants us to assume responsibility for our own wrong attitudes and actions. Most of the time, you won't change other people's views on what they've done. You won't convince them to suddenly apologize for their mistake or return what they've taken. You have no control over them. You do have control over *your* response, however.

There is also the possibility that God's perspective on the matter differs from yours. Remember these words of Jesus: "Why do you look at the speck of sawdust in your brother's eye and pay no attention to the plank in your own eye?" (Matthew 7:3). The Lord wants us to deal with our own issues. That means owning up to our sin, regardless of who is "most wrong."

Adjust Your Focus

As we talked about when we examined the issue of guilt, when we're hurt by someone, it's easy to focus on the offender and what he or she has done. Yet the Lord doesn't want us to dwell on that person's sin. He knows that in a time of pain, we need more than ever to keep our focus on Him. As David wrote, "I will extol the LORD at all times; his praise will always be on my lips" (Psalm 34:1). It's hard to hold onto bitterness when we are praising God!

Get your focus on God and you will be one step closer to forgiveness.

Abandon Your Desire to Get Even

Several years ago, a woman wrote that her husband of two years had an affair with a young widow, who then carried his child. The wife was devastated and angry. She wanted to kill her husband and the widow. Yet she knew this wasn't the answer to her troubles. Instead she prayed to God, and the Lord gave her the strength to forgive both the husband and the widow.

The baby was born in the home of the husband and wife and raised as their own. He turned out to be their only child. In fifty years, the couple never discussed the incident again. "But," the wife wrote, "I've read the love and gratitude in His eyes a thousand times."[4]

Jesus gave us the same example during his time on earth. As Peter described, "He did not retaliate when he was insulted. When he suffered, he did not threaten to get even. He left his case in the hands of God, who always judges fairly" (1 Peter 2:23 NLT).

Scripture is not ambivalent about our duty when we are wronged. We must abandon our desire to get even or take revenge: "Don't insist on getting even; that's not for you to do. 'I'll do the judging,' says God. 'I'll take care of it'" (Romans 12:19 MSG). Let it go and leave it to Him. It's not just the Christian thing to do. It's also in our best interest.

Ask God to Use You

If you've worked through the progression above, you're ready for the next step—asking God to use you to bless your offender. Is it easy to seek blessing for someone who has wronged you? Of course not. But it's exactly what the Lord requires that we do.

Paul wrote, "Bless those who persecute you; bless and do not curse…Do not repay anyone evil for evil. Be careful to do what is right in the eyes of everybody. If it is possible, as far as it depends on you, live at peace with everyone…Do not be overcome by evil, but overcome evil with good" (Romans 12:14–21). It's not just a matter of making a wise choice. It's a question of choosing good or evil. We must decide to fall on the side of good.

Act in Obedience

During World War II, Corrie ten Boom and her sister, Betsie, had been prisoners at Ravensbruck, a concentration camp. Corrie survived her incarceration and the intolerable conditions; Betsie did not. In 1947, two years after the end of the war, Corrie returned to Germany to deliver the message that God forgives. She had finished speaking at a church in Germany when a heavyset man in a gray overcoat moved through the departing crowd to speak to Corrie.

Suddenly, Corrie recognized the man. She pictured him as she had known him before: wearing a blue uniform and a visored cap with skull and crossbones, a leather crop swinging from his belt. He had been one of the most merciless guards at Ravensbruck. She was face-to-face with one of her tormentors.

The man, who clearly did not recognize Corrie, explained his past and that he was now a Christian. He thrust his hand out and said, "Fraulein, will you forgive me?"

Corrie recorded her response.

It could not have been many seconds that he stood there—hand held out—but to me it seemed hours as I wrestled with the most difficult thing I ever had to do.

For I had to do it—I knew that. The message that God forgives has a prior condition: that we forgive those who have injured us. "If you do not forgive men their trespasses," Jesus says, "neither will your Father in heaven forgive your trespasses."

So, woodenly and mechanically, I thrust my hand into the one stretched out to me. And as I did, an incredible thing took place. The current started in my shoulder, raced down my arm, and sprang into our joined hands. And then this healing warmth seemed to flood my whole being, bringing tears to my eyes.

"I forgive you, brother!" I cried. "With all my heart."[5]

Corrie ten Boom had no desire to forgive the Ravensbruck guard. She lacked any feeling of forgiveness. Yet she understood that forgiveness is not a feeling but an act of obedience to the prompting of the Holy Spirit. Scripture says, "Since we live by the Spirit, let us keep in step with the Spirit" (Galatians 5:25). When we put aside our feelings and obediently stretch out our hands to forgive, we move in God's will, enabling Him to forgive us and wipe away the stain of bitterness on our hearts.

Forgiveness changes everything.

Time to Settle Up

Let's say that you've worked through the progression above. You know that you need to let go of your bitterness. You know you need forgiveness for your bitter feelings and that you need to forgive. You *want* to forgive so you can renew your heart and move on with your life.

What now?

It's time to settle up with the Lord. First, I recommend that you review Matthew 18:21–35, the parable about the servant who refuses to show mercy to a fellow servant. Through the parable, Jesus is telling us that we will be forgiven as we forgive others. Next, find a quiet place for a prayer time with the Lord. Make a full confession—hold nothing back. Ask God to forgive you for harboring ill feelings in your heart. *Know* that He will forgive you. *Accept* that forgiveness! *Ask* for His grace to forgive the person that has offended you. Your heart will find joy, relief, and freedom.

Are you done? Not quite. If the person or people who wronged you have asked you to forgive them and you refused or ignored their request, you must go to them and offer your forgiveness. You must take responsibility for your bitterness and lack of forgiveness—even if they refuse to acknowledge their own culpability.

You also need to ask yourself if your bitterness has led you into further sin against others. If so, and if the offender or others are aware of it, once again, you need to go to those people and ask for forgiveness.

I'm not talking about a situation where you're envious of your neighbor Fred's new Porsche. Yes, that's an attitude that can lead to bitterness, but it's a private matter between you and God. On the other hand, if you become so bitter that you complain to everyone you meet about how Fred flaunts his wealth, you need to confess your sin to Fred and to everyone you've spoken to and seek their forgiveness.

It isn't easy to confess to a bitter attitude and ask for forgiveness. It's important to be careful in how you handle the situation. Don't, for example, lead off by saying, "If I have offended you in some way, I hope you'll forgive me." That's not enough! Offer a full confession, and be specific: "Fred, I've been bitter about your new Porsche, and since then I've trashed you in three conversations with neighbors. I've sinned against you. I'm sorry about what I've done. Will you forgive me?"

Fred may forgive you, and he may not. If not, don't use your newfound spiritual wisdom to try to convince him otherwise or show him the error of his ways. Leave it to God to work on his heart. Don't feel you have to keep going back to obtain his forgiveness, either. The good news is that once you've done the hard work of confessing your sin to God, securing His forgiveness, and taking steps when needed to offer and seek the forgiveness of others, your responsibility is complete. You're done. And your heart, at last, is free.

UNCLE BOB

I've already described the hold that bitterness had on my Uncle Bob after his brother cheated him out of the inheritance from his mother. Now I'll share the rest of Bob's story.

A few years after my grandmother died and my other uncle disappeared, Bob's health declined significantly. I have no doubt that the toll from bitterness contributed to his worsening condition. Bob wound up in the hospital. He was dying.

I was the pastor at a church about thirteen miles from Bob's home and was the closest family member. For weeks, at all hours of the day, I received frequent calls from the hospital: "It doesn't look like your uncle is going to make it through the night. You'd better come over." Yet each time after I made that drive, Bob would rally and recover enough to see another day.

Bob wasn't a believer. When I tried to talk to him about his salvation, however, he always waved me away. He didn't want to talk about it.

Finally, during one of my unplanned visits, I confronted my uncle. "Bob, you know you're going to die one of these days," I said. "The Lord in His grace has spared you this long. You've got to get right with Him. Why won't you?"

This time Bob answered me. "I can't," he said. "It's because of the bitterness I have toward Ma and Eldon. I hate 'em. I can't expect God to forgive me if I won't forgive them."

"You can forgive them," I said. "You can let that out right now."

Bob lay quietly in bed for a few moments. Then he said in a low voice, "I have to go to the cemetery. I have to ask for Ma's forgiveness."

"Bob, you can't leave the hospital now."

"I've gotta go."

It was a crazy idea. But as we talked about it and I considered it, I thought, *Why not? It doesn't matter if he dies here or in my car. Let's load him up.*

It took some convincing, but I secured permission from the hospital to transport Bob in my old blue Cadillac. He sat in the backseat with his wheelchair, oxygen tank, and a pan that he spit up in several times. We didn't say a word on the drive to the cemetery.

I located my grandmother's tombstone, wheeled Bob over to the spot, then walked a few paces away. He sat there quietly, his body shaking. Finally, I heard his voice: "Ma! I forgive you! This is Bob."

That was it. I helped my uncle back into the car, and began the return drive to the hospital. Suddenly Bob broke the silence. "Denny," he said, "how good a liar are you? At my funeral, could you say something nice about me? Tell 'em I was a pretty good guy?"

"Bob," I said, "the nicest thing I can say at someone's funeral is that they knew Jesus Christ as their personal Savior. Can I say that about you?"

There was no answer for a few minutes. Then Bob said, "Now you can." My uncle died a few days later, and I presided over the funeral.

Bitterness will destroy your heart. Forgiveness will free it. Don't allow your life and relationships to be poisoned by bitterness. Don't walk into eternity with a bucketful of bitterness in your heart. Get right with the Lord, starting today. You won't regret it.

A Thought to Remember

Unforgiveness is like drinking poison and waiting for the other person to die.

A Verse to Review

"See to it that no one misses the grace of God and that no bitter root grows up to cause trouble and defile many."

HEBREWS 12:15

A Question for Reflection

Who do you need to forgive from the heart?

CHAPTER FIVE

FREEING THE ANXIOUS HEART

INTERNAL: OUR RELATIONSHIP WITH OURSELVES

"Anxiety is a thin stream of fear trickling through the mind. If encouraged, it cuts a channel into which all other thoughts are drained."

ADAPTED FROM A. S. ROCHE

Do you worry? Are you stressed and anxious? A pilot named Gregg Warren may have the solution to your problems. The idea is to write down your worries on a piece of paper, burn the paper, and send him the ashes. Then, for just $5, Warren will toss your ashes out of his plane over the town of Carefree, Arizona. Most likely, the ashes will actually come down somewhere in New Mexico, but the important thing is that they're released over Carefree. At that point, presumably, you'll be free of your worries forever.

Sounds silly, you say? It wasn't to the five thousand people who paid Warren $25,000 during the first six months of his business.[1] Other than easing Mr. Warren's financial concerns, I doubt anyone involved achieved a lasting change in their stress levels. The story is a sign, though, of how pervasive the problem of anxiety is today.

We are a stressed-out people. Technology pushes us to move at a faster pace. Economic upheaval threatens our jobs and our security. War and other conflicts abroad demand our attention. The threat of terrorist attack, when we travel and even when we're at home, is a disturbing addition to our ever-increasing list of concerns.

The results are apparent. *Harvard Business Review* has reported that stress-related symptoms account for 60 to 90 percent of medical office visits.[2] Anxiety disorders as a group are the most common mental illnesses in the United States, with more than 40 million adults affected by these debilitating illnesses each year.[3] At least one recent survey showed that a third of the U.S. population experienced a panic attack during the previous twelve months.[4]

One person who understands that terrifying feeling is Lori Mangrum, a mother in Indiana. She still remembers the night she woke up in her bedroom gasping for breath, her heart racing. When she tried to stand, nausea overwhelmed her, and she collapsed on the floor. It was another in a series of debilitating panic attacks. They got so bad that she couldn't even drive to the grocery store.

A physician eventually discovered that Lori had a heart condition that contributed to the attacks. But that wasn't the only cause of Lori's anxiety. For years, she had been a "fixer," always working to solve other people's problems and ignoring her own. The physician recommended therapy and anti-anxiety medication.[5]

You may not be dealing with panic attacks, but we're all familiar with feelings of stress. Our physical and emotional condition certainly contributes to our anxiety level. When we're deeply worried and stressed out, we can ease our burden through exercise, better diet choices, and confronting the causes of our emotional duress. Sometimes we are simply trying to do too much, and cutting back on activities brings some relief.

No matter how hard we work to reduce stress in our lives, however, we'll never succeed in eliminating it. Even when we're at our best physically and emotionally, the next crisis is always just around the corner. A relationship falls apart. A job is down-sized. An illness attacks unexpectedly. A close relative dies. We can't escape the inevitable calamities that are part of life. As Jesus said, "In this world you will have trouble" (John 16:33). And when trouble strikes, our hearts are so often ensnared by feelings of anxiety.

You can take steps to lower the stress in your life. Ultimately, however, the solution to freeing an anxious heart is not physical or emotional. It's spiritual.

PAY ATTENTION TO THE TENSION

Merriam-Webster defines anxiety as "painful or apprehensive uneasiness of mind usually over an impending or anticipated ill." A dictionary definition for worry is "to torment oneself by disturbing thoughts." When we're anxious and worried, we turn our focus away from the present and toward what is coming—or what *may* be coming. As Mark Twain once said, "I've seen many troubles in my lifetime, only half of which ever came true."

The English word *worry* comes from the Anglo-Saxon word meaning "to strangle" or "to choke." Worry and anxiety choke the life out of us. They are a waste of time, thought, and energy. They spoil our dispositions, damage our relationships, and steal our optimism.

Max Lucado has described worry and its effect on our thought life:

Worry divides the mind. The biblical word for worry (*merimnao*) is a compound of two Greek words: *merizo* (to divide) and *nous* (the mind). Anxiety splits our energy between today's priorities and tomorrow's problems. Part of the mind is on the now; the rest is on the not yet. The result is half-minded living.

There's a problem when we divide our thoughts this way. If half of our thinking is on getting by in the present and the other half is spent worrying about the future, we crowd out the One who should be the real center of our attention. Anxiety is a sign that we've taken things into our own hands rather than trust in the Lord.

A friend once told me, "Pay attention to the tension." It was wise advice. If we have tension in our lives, it means we're flying solo. We've shoved the Lord out of the captain's chair and are attempting to act as pilot, copilot, and control tower, all at the same time. Guess what? If you keep that up, you're headed for a crash.

Here's what happens when you and I push God aside and allow anxiety to rule our hearts:

- We become the center of our universe. We're not free because "it's all about me."

- We deny Christ's power and promises. Jesus says, "Do not worry, saying, 'What shall we eat?' or 'What shall we drink?' or 'What shall we wear?' For the pagans run after all these things, and your heavenly Father knows that you need them. But seek first his kingdom and his righteousness, and all these things will be given to you as well" (Matthew 6:31–33).
- We forget our personal relationship with the Father. We are not orphans! He will support the life He gives.
- We abandon our faith. Jesus is talking to worriers when he addresses "you of little faith" (Matthew 6:30).
- We become distracted and divided. Our focus is on potential problems instead of the Lord.

I know that worry is unhealthy, you say. *I know God doesn't want me to do it. I know it's a spiritual issue. But I can't seem to stop. What am I supposed to do?*

Let the Great Physician prescribe the remedy.

GOD'S ANTIDOTE FOR ANXIETY

Scripture is clear about the Lord's antidote for anxiety. It is presented to us through the words of the apostle Paul in his letter to the Philippians:

Do not be anxious about anything, but in everything, by prayer and petition, with thanksgiving, present your requests to God. And the peace of God, which transcends all understanding, will guard your hearts and your minds in Christ Jesus. (Philippians 4:6–7)

Fortunately for us, this life-changing passage of Scripture does not stop with the words *Do not be anxious about anything.* We are given not only a command, but also the means to obey the command: *in everything, by prayer and petition, with thanksgiving, present your requests to God.* The message can be paraphrased this way: Pray about and give thanks for *everything!*

God desires a relationship with you. He wants to hear from you—not just during times of crisis, but during the mundane moments of your day. Nothing is too small to trouble Him about. If it's big enough to bother you, it's big enough to talk to Him about it. As Peter says, "Give all your worries and cares to God, for he cares about what happens to you" (1 Peter 5:7 NLT). Notice Peter doesn't say "just the big worries." His instruction is to pass on *all* your worries to the Lord.

Most of us understand that there is value in prayer. We want to spend time with the Lord. We mean well. Yet somehow, in the crush of daily responsibilities, God gets put on hold. Too often, the best we seem to do is an "arrow" prayer before we climb into bed at the end of another exhausting and stressful day: "Lord, please help me finish my project on time tomorrow. Thanks. Amen."

God wants more than that. If we want to experience His power, presence, and peace in our lives, *we* need more than that.

I know it isn't easy, but I recommend carving out a regular time each day for conversation with the Lord. Early morning, before the demands and distractions of the day begin, is often most effective. If that sounds like a challenge, start small. Even ten or fifteen minutes with the Lord when you first get up can set the right tone for the rest of your day. Tell Him about what's on your mind. Share your concerns and frustrations. Realize that nothing is too great for His power, and nothing is too small for His fatherly care. Remember also to listen for His response. When you quiet your heart and mind long enough, you will hear His answer.

> *Nothing is too great for God's power, and nothing is too small for His fatherly care.*

Your prayer time need not end in the morning. Why not continue the conversation over the rest of the day? The Lord is not someone we leave at home in our "prayer closet." He is with us every place, every moment: "Surely I am with you always, to the very end of the age" (Matthew 28:20). We can pray about our troubles at the very moment they happen and be reassured that He hears what's on our hearts and has our best interests in mind.

AN ATTITUDE OF GRATITUDE

There's another requirement to Paul's admonition to pray: "…in everything, by prayer and petition, *with thanksgiving* [emphasis mine], present your requests to

God." We must do more than commit time to pray. We must also commit to the proper approach to prayer. We'll find peace if we address the Lord with an attitude of gratitude.

Most of us are great complainers and gripers. When we're at a restaurant, we don't like waiting for our dinner to be served. We don't like it if the food is cold when it arrives. And heaven help the poor waitress if we find a fly in our soup!

Some of us can find something wrong with everyone we meet and everything we experience. It's as if we've taken God's antidote for anxiety and turned it on is head:

> Do not be calm about anything, but in everything, by dwelling on it constantly and feeling picked on by God, with thoughts like "and this is the thanks I get," present your aggravations to everyone you know but Him. And the acid in your stomach, which transcends all milk products, will cause you an ulcer and the doctor bills will cause you a heart attack and you will lose your mind.[6]

This isn't how the Lord wants us to live! Rather, Scripture tells us to "Be joyful always; pray continually; give thanks in all circumstances, for this is God's will for you in Christ Jesus" (1 Thessalonians 5:16–18).

All circumstances. Not just the good days, but the days when you lose your job, when your kids yell at you, when you're handed a speeding ticket. You may not be able to see it yet, but God will find a way to make good use of your present trouble. When we trust Him to do that and thank Him even for our hardships, we find our hearts moving toward a place of peace.

When we adopt an attitude of gratitude, we find:

- It adjusts our outlook on life.
- It brings our will into harmony with God's will.
- It affirms God's sovereignty, love, and wisdom.
- It pleases God.
- It releases the generosity of God.
- It reminds us of the past.
- It defeats the enemy.

- It dissipates fear and anxiety.
- It relaxes us.
- It is a statement of faith.

What does this look like in real life? Here's an example. Matthew Henry, the eighteenth-century English clergyman and author, was robbed one night. He later wrote in his journal, "Let me be thankful—first, because I was never robbed before; second, because although they took my wallet, they did not take my life; third, because although they took my all, it was not much; and fourth, because it was I who was robbed, not I who robbed."[7]

That is an attitude of gratitude, and is the kind of perspective God asks of each of us.

Incorporating a thankful attitude does not come easily or naturally to most of us. To improve your "thank you" reflex, I suggest giving thanks to the Lord for His love, provision, blessings, and guidance whenever you pray. You also might make a daily practice of writing down the things you are thankful for in your life. Do it after your prayer time in the morning, during a coffee break at work, or just before bed. Those little reminders can make a big difference in our attitude.

My attitude of gratitude was lacking some years ago on the day I was in Brazil and flew to meet an old and dear friend in São Paulo. I expected to have just a couple of hours with him, but I was eagerly looking forward to it. After I got off the plane at the São Paulo airport, I found myself stuck in a long line, waiting for my passport to be checked. The line wasn't moving. I checked my watch, clenched my jaw, and fumed. I really wanted to see my friend, and our time was slipping away. I began to think, *Who in this line can I push out of the way?*

I realized my thoughts were running out of control. I took a deep breath. *Okay, Dennis, what's going on here?* I thought. *You're angry and anxious. Is this how the Lord wants you to handle this situation?*

I recognized that there wasn't much I could do about the slow-moving line. I remembered that God is in control. I recalled the Lord's command to be anxious for nothing, to pray about everything, and to give thanks in every situation. So, right there in line, I prayed to the Lord and thanked Him for my life at that moment and for whatever He had planned for me. Slowly, I felt the tension drain from my body. It was replaced by a wonderful sensation of peace.

A few moments later, a woman standing next to me in line spoke up. I'd been so wrapped up in my problems I hadn't even noticed her. "Excuse me, sir," she said. "Can I ask you a question? This may sound a little strange, but do you believe in angels?"

I was surprised by the question. "Yes," I said. "But why do you ask?"

"I see a lot of light around you," she said.

Now I was even more surprised. "Any light you see around me is Jesus Christ," I said. "He's the light of the world."

We began a discussion about faith. This woman was an author who traveled around the world speaking about the New Age movement. Yet she seemed to be sincerely seeking God. We had a wonderful conversation and I had the opportunity later to send her material about angels. It was clear from letters she sent back that God was working in her heart.

If I hadn't followed the Lord's prescription for anxiety that day in line, I would have endured a miserable afternoon and missed an opportunity to share His truth. How many other opportunities have I missed over the years? Too many to count, I'm sure. But during that moment, at least, I obeyed the counsel the apostle Paul gives to all of us: "Let the peace of Christ rule in your hearts…And be thankful" (Colossians 3:15).

I Will Glorify Your Name

There's one more important and very effective way to cultivate an attitude of gratitude: worship. The Lord clearly desires our adoration. He knows it is for our benefit. As Jesus said, "A time is coming and has now come when the true worshipers will worship the Father in spirit and truth, for they are the kind of worshipers the Father seeks" (John 4:23). When we get in the habit of regularly praising God for His love and provision, we move the focus away from ourselves and our problems and onto the source of our joy and peace. As author and pastor Rick Warren wrote, "When God is at the center, you worship. When He's not,

> *"Worry is the warning light that God has been shoved to the sideline."*

you worry. Worry is the warning light that God has been shoved to the sideline."[8]

Worship is the full extension of a thankful heart. David wrote, "Teach me your way, O LORD, and I will walk in your truth; give me an undivided heart, that I may fear your name. I will praise you, O LORD my God, with all my heart; I will glorify your name forever" (Psalm 86:11–12). When we fill our hearts with praise, there's no room for worry and anxiety.

Worship connects us to God's peace by enhancing our prayer life. When Jesus taught the disciples how to pray, he began with words of praise: "Our Father in heaven, hallowed be your name" (Matthew 6:9). As our conversations with the Lord grow longer and deeper, we understand just how capable He is of taking care of us and our troubles. Our problems seem less imposing. The anxiety falls away. Our trust in Him grows. And we discover the joy Paul talked about in Scripture: "Rejoice in the Lord always. I will say it again: Rejoice!" (Philippians 4:4).

REMEMBER HIS PROMISE

What happens when we apply the Lord's antidote for anxiety to our lives? The answer is right there in Scripture: "And the peace of God, which transcends all understanding, will guard your hearts and your minds in Christ Jesus" (Philippians 4:7).

We're talking here about a profound peace, a supernatural peace, standing guard over our hearts. Picture Jesus as a sentinel, striding back and forth before the portal of our inner life, blocking the path of all intruders. He knows that "A heart at peace gives life to the body" (Proverbs 14:30). He won't let anything interfere with that peace. That's the peace we want and need every day of our lives. It's the peace that is more powerful than any crisis we'll ever face.

Remember Lori Mangrum, the Indiana mother who struggled with panic attacks? Through therapy with a Christian counselor, she discovered that she continually tried to fix others' problems because it made her feel loved and accepted. She wanted to be seen as strong and competent. On the inside, however, her stress level was shooting off the chart. She was far from the Lord's peace. She lived daily with an anxious heart.

Lori recalls the turning point:

I was driving home one afternoon following a session with my counselor, feeling so overwhelmed at the reality of my situation and utterly hopeless. I cried out to God, "I can't do this alone, it's too hard. If you're really there, then show me, and I will trust you!" In the stillness God's answer was clear: "Trust me first—then I will show you." And he did.[9]

Lori realized that the Lord never intended for her to be strong and competent every moment. She began focusing more on pleasing Him instead of everyone else. The panic attacks, and her fear of the attacks, began to diminish. Slowly, she began to rediscover the joy and peace of an untroubled heart.

You will have trouble in this life. I can guarantee it. But that doesn't mean you have to settle for an anxious existence. God offers you so much more. If you trust Him with your concerns, you'll discover a Friend greater than your worst problem. Remember His instruction and promise: Don't be anxious about anything. Pray about everything. Pray with thanksgiving. When you do, He will stand guard over your heart and mind, and grant you peace.

Does that make more sense than tossing ashes over a town in Arizona? I think so too.

A THOUGHT TO REMEMBER

Pay attention to the tension!

A VERSE TO REVIEW

"Cast all your anxiety on him because he cares for you."

1 PETER 5:7

A QUESTION FOR REFLECTION

Will you apply God's antidote for your anxiety?

CHAPTER SIX

DEFENDING THE FREE HEART

"Do not be far from me, O Lord. Awake, and rise to my defense!"

PSALM 35:22–23

On his drive to work early that morning, U.S. Air Corps Lt. Kermit Tyler listened to a local station playing Hawaiian music. He was surprised; the station normally didn't begin broadcasting until 7 A.M. But Tyler knew the station sometimes broadcast ahead of schedule as an aid to incoming squadrons of B-17 bombers, which used the signal as a homing beacon. Unconcerned, Tyler drove on to his assignment—his second day on the job as pursuit officer at the Fort Shafter Information Center, on the Hawaiian island of Oahu, at an installation called Pearl Harbor.

The date was December 7, 1941.

A few minutes after 7 that morning, Tyler received a call from a private working a radar station on Oahu's Opana Point. The private sounded excited. He reported a huge incoming blip on his oscilloscope, the largest he'd ever seen. Tyler remembered the early radio broadcast. He knew that a squadron of B-17s would make a big impression. He was the only officer on duty at the time. There was no one to confer with.

"Don't worry about it," he told the private. "It's okay."

Nearly an hour later, Tyler stepped outside for a short break and a breath of tropical air. He looked to the west. The sky was filling with incoming planes and puffs of smoke. Only then did it begin to dawn on him. The enemy had launched a sneak attack. He had made a terrible mistake.[1]

If you have been living with a troubled heart, it's my prayer that our discussion so far has helped you identify the source of that trouble and enabled you to invite the Lord to change your heart. A heart free of guilt, bitterness, and worry, beating in time with the will of God, is as close to heaven as we can get on this earth. It's where we all want and need to be. If your heart is free, I am thrilled for you. Congratulations!

Along with those congratulations, however, I must add a warning. You see, you are now a target of the enemy, and he is planning a sneak attack even as we speak. The last thing Satan wants is an untroubled believer acting in step with the promptings of the Holy Spirit. The enemy is silent and swift. He will do everything he can to confuse you, to disrupt holy lines of communication, and to assault your position as a warrior for the Lord. If you relax your guard, he will strike a deadly blow.

To stay free and untroubled, you must be alert and fortify your position. You must prepare to defend your heart.

GUARD YOUR HEART DILIGENTLY

When someone tells you to do something "above all else," you know it must be important. I used to own a maroon '65 Thunderbird. This T-Bird was a beauty and a personal favorite. My daughter Jennifer was sixteen at the time and had just learned how to drive. She asked one evening if she could take the Thunderbird to meet some friends. The T-Bird was a big vehicle, and we had a small garage. I said yes to Jennifer and asked her to drive safely, then added, "Above all else, be careful when you back out of the driveway. It's a tight space and you've got to watch."

You can guess what happened. Just a few minutes later, Jennifer came into the house, tears running down her cheeks. She had torn the siding off the garage with the T-Bird's big bumper. Somehow, my words of wisdom hadn't penetrated. Now we were both sorry!

Solomon, writing in the book of Proverbs, passes on his wisdom about the Lord and practical living to the next generation. I can imagine him sitting in a place of honor, conversing with a young man, perhaps a teenager like my daughter. If teens back then were anything like teens today, they may not have been that interested in the words of an old man, even if he was a king. I picture this particular young man before Solomon, one ear tuned to the king's words, the rest of his thoughts drifting toward what he's going to do that evening. But Solomon knows how important this instruction is. He captures the young man's focus by speaking in a loud, firm voice:

> My son, pay attention to what I say; listen closely to my words. Do not let them out of your sight, keep them within your heart; for they are life to those who find them and health to a man's whole body. Above all else, guard your heart, for it is the wellspring of life. (Proverbs 4:20–23)

What does Solomon advise this young man—and all of us—to do above all else? *To guard our hearts.* The heart is the gateway to our emotions and relationships, yet most of us monitor the oil levels in our cars more carefully than we watch over our hearts. It was Thomas Watson who said, "A wandering heart needs a watchful eye."[2] We must be diligent in watching over and guarding our hearts.

The heart is the "wellspring of life." What flows from its spring will determine the story of our lives. It is the source of what we need to survive and thrive. We must keep that source from deadly contamination. If we don't, our wellspring will spew out manipulation, deception, and seduction. Just as a town's citizens rely on a pure water supply to stay healthy, so do we rely on pure hearts to experience joyful, healthy lives.

The heart is the gateway to our emotions and relationships.

John Eldredge has written, "[God's command] doesn't say guard your heart because it's criminal; it says guard your heart because it is the wellspring of your life, because it is a *treasure*, because everything else depends on it."[3] All you have done to free your heart will be lost if you fail to guard your heart.

SPARKS OF EVIL

Author Dallas Willard has written, "When our heart comes to new life in God, the old programs are still running contrary to our new heart."[4] Bad habits die hard. We may have to consciously turn away from our usual past tendencies in order to keep a pure and free heart. You can be sure that Satan will move quickly to test you. Be ready!

Willard has also written, "There remains in us a spark of evil that can be fanned into a flame if we are not watchful. We are still recovering sinners!" No matter how long we've been a Christian and how close we are to God, we are still human. We are always capable of sin. Even a faint ember can be fanned into a roaring forest fire under the right conditions. We must be careful.

Let's get practical. What does it mean to guard your heart? What are the weak spots that our enemy will seek to attack? In Scripture, Jesus specifically uses the word *guard* in His teaching on five danger areas. Here is a look at each one.

- FALSE TEACHING: "Be on your guard against the yeast of the Pharisees and Sadducees" (Matthew 16:6). Jesus wasn't talking about baking here, but about some of the common beliefs and practices of the time. The Pharisees were legalists, so committed to following the rules that they often missed the spirit of the Lord's laws. The Sadducees, meanwhile, interpreted God's laws so liberally that they denied fundamentals such as the resurrection and the existence of angels. Today, either extreme is still dangerous.
- GREED: "Be on your guard against all kinds of greed" (Luke 12:15). We live in a world that encourages a greedy attitude. Advertisements on television, in magazines, and on the Internet bombard us with messages telling us to buy, buy, buy. *I need more,* we think. *I deserve more. I need a new wardrobe. A better car. A bigger house. I need what he's got.* Whenever your thoughts drift in this direction, you're letting down your guard.
- DECEPTION: "For false Christs and false prophets will appear and perform signs and miracles to deceive the elect—if that were possible. So be on your guard" (Mark 13:22–23). When someone presents a statement to you as truth, whether it's a matter of Scripture or anything else, examine it with a critical eye. Does it ring true? Does it square with the Word of God? We are a gullible people. Be wary of the enemy's attempts at deception.

- SPIRITUAL SLACKNESS: "Be on guard! Be alert! You do not know when that time will come" (Mark 13:33). There may be moments when we sense that our usefulness to the Lord has ended or that Christ's return is imminent. We can use either as an excuse to stop growing in faith and to ease up on guarding our hearts. We may decide we don't need to pray as often, read our Bibles, or go to church. But only the Lord knows what the future holds, when our time on earth will end, when Christ will return, and what purposes He still has for us. Our job is to remain spiritually strong, to keep growing in faith, and to stay obedient to the Lord's will.

- DESTRUCTIVE ACTIONS AND ATTITUDES: "Be on guard, so that your hearts will not be weighted down with dissipation and drunkenness and the worries of life" (Luke 21:34 NASB). The enemy will throw all manner of obstacles in your path. He'll attempt to remove Christian friends from your life. He'll tempt you with drink, drugs, illicit sex, dishonest means to money, or whatever vice most appeals to you. He'll send disease and other hardships your way in hopes of making you anxious. If you're not careful, you will respond with damaging actions and attitudes that will again ensnare your heart. You must remember who has the power and who you belong to.

A chain is only as strong as its weakest link. Which of these danger areas are you most susceptible to? Are there others where Satan has a good chance to "break" you? Take a few minutes right now to look at the target—you—from the enemy's point of view. What strategy is he most likely considering? Where are you most vulnerable to a sneak attack?

Years ago, a pastor and longtime friend of mine developed a problem with alcohol. It started out with a single glass of wine on Sunday nights to help George relax after a full weekend of ministry. Little by little, the amount of alcohol increased until it became a serious issue. The Lord, by His grace, enabled George to deal with his problem at a heart level, and he has been free of alcohol dependence for several years.

George now knows his vulnerability to alcohol and understands that Satan knows it too. That's why today he will not drink even one glass of wine, including on social occasions. George also realizes that he is most vulnerable to the enemy's attacks when he is alone and spiritually and emotionally depleted. Now, when George travels, he has another man join him who supports him in prayer and who George can share openly with and be accountable to. He is very aware that there remains in him a spark of evil that can easily be fanned into a flame.

The better you know the strengths and weaknesses of your personality and temperament, the better you can plan an effective defense and guard your heart. Awareness of your enemy and yourself is a powerful weapon. As Scripture says, "Take heed, and guard your life diligently, lest you forget the things which your eyes have seen, and lest they depart from your [mind and] heart all the days of your life" (Deuteronomy 4:9 AMP).

There's a reason why I use so much war imagery when discussing these issues: we are at war with the forces of darkness. To win this spiritual conflict, we must get ready. We must dress for battle.

THE ARMOR OF GOD

The apostle Paul's letter to the Ephesians makes clear what we are up against and how we can best prepare to defeat the enemy:

> Finally, be strong in the Lord and in his mighty power. Put on the full armor of God so that you can take your stand against the devil's schemes. For our struggle is not against flesh and blood, but against the rulers, against the authorities, against the powers of this dark world and against the spiritual forces of evil in the heavenly realms. Therefore put on the full armor of God, so that when the day of evil comes, you may be able to stand your ground, and after you have done everything, to stand. Stand firm then, with the belt of truth buckled around your waist, with the breastplate of righteousness in place, and with your feet fitted with the readiness that comes from the gospel of peace. In addition to all this, take up the shield of faith with which you can extinguish all the flaming arrows of the evil one. Take the helmet of salvation and the sword of the Spirit, which is the word of God. And pray in the Spirit on all occasions with all kinds of prayers and requests. With this in mind, be alert and always keep on praying for all the saints." (Ephesians 6:10–18)

Can you hear the call to arms and smell the smoke of battle? In this war, there are no conscientious objectors, draft dodgers, or spiritual pacifists. Like it or not, you are in the fight. Your heart is already under attack. That's why you'd better prepare yourself by adorning the proper armor.

The Belt of Truth

What does Paul mean when he says, "Stand firm then, with the belt of truth buckled around your waist" (v. 14)? As a Roman citizen, Paul was familiar with the attire of a Roman soldier. The belt or girdle was six to eight inches wide and was fastened around the waist. It was the foundation of a soldier's battle dress because everything else was attached to it. If the belt was not in place, the armor was not secure.

The belt of truth is a symbol for the "word of truth" (2 Timothy 2:15; James 1:18; Psalm 119:42–43) and the "Spirit of truth" (John 14:17; 16:13). It is God's Word found in Scripture that is inspired by the Holy Spirit. We can depend on God to reveal what is right, good, and just through His Word. Truth exposes Satan's deceiving ways and his evil intentions. When your faith is solid and your knowledge of and obedience to the Word is complete, Satan will not be able to move you.

The Breastplate of Righteousness

Paul also exhorts us to "Stand firm…with the breastplate of righteousness in place" (v. 14). A Roman soldier's breastplate was made of bronze and backed with a tough piece of hide. It was like a knight's coat of mail, covering the soldier's front and back from the neck to the thighs. It protected the vital organs, where a wound could be fatal.

When Paul says to put on the breastplate of righteousness, he is telling us to remember that God declares us righteous. He takes away our sin and through His grace gives us His righteousness. It does not depend on our actions. Instead, "This righteousness from God comes through faith in Jesus Christ to all who believe" (Romans 3:22). When the enemy attacks us with accusations designed to push us back into guilt, depression, despair, and destruction, we can protect our hearts by consistently acknowledging the gift and power of God's right-eousness.

The Shoes of Peace

You might be surprised at the third vital piece of equipment on Paul's list: shoes. He says, "Stand firm... with your feet fitted with the readiness that comes from the gospel of peace" (v. 15).

The shoes of a Roman soldier were actually open-toed leather boots, with a heavily studded sole tied by straps to the ankles and shins. These were not tennis shoes. They were made of hardy material, designed for any road or weather condition. Most important, they provided good traction. When a soldier was assaulted, he didn't want his feet sliding in the dirt. An enemy would try to knock him off his feet. In hand-to-hand combat, sure footing was essential.

Our enemy also tries to knock us off our feet. His tactic is to encourage us to slip into worry. If he can keep us focused on problems with our spouse, our kids, our health, the bills, or our job, we will eventually lose our balance and leave our hearts open to more devastating blows. Our sure footing comes from the "gospel of peace"—our acceptance of what God has done for us. As Jesus said, "I have told you these things, so that in me you may have peace" (John 16:33).

The Shield of Faith

What else do we need as we dress for battle? Paul's next instruction is to "take up the shield of faith with which you can extinguish all the flaming arrows of the evil one" (v. 16). A Roman soldier's shield was impressive, four feet tall and two-and-a-half-feet wide. It consisted of two layers of laminated wood, covered first with linen and then with hide, and bound on top and bottom with iron. An iron ornament decorated the front. A man could put his entire body behind his shield and safely allow it to absorb the tips of javelins and arrows.

One of the enemy's most dangerous weapons, however, was the fiery dart. He dipped this small arrow in pitch, set it on fire, and launched it at the soldiers. To counteract the fire from these darts, Roman soldiers soaked their shields in water. In battle, a soldier's shield might be covered with these small arrows, steam rising from each as the water extinguished the fire.

We also must contend with an assortment of flaming arrows. Satan launches repeated volleys of fire-tipped weapons: rumors and lies, material and sexual temptations, dissatisfaction and conflicts with Christian brothers and sisters. Unless we have a stout shield of faith, those weapons will find their mark. Faith itself is not our protection. Rather, our shield is the *object* of our faith: God's person (Genesis 15:1; Psalm 84:11), promises (1 Kings 8:56; Romans 4:20), and providence (Romans 8:28). That is armor no flaming arrow can penetrate.

The Helmet of Salvation

Our battle dress will not be complete unless we don the "helmet of salvation" (v. 17). A Roman soldier's helmet had a wide metal band to protect the forehead and plates for the cheeks. It extended down several inches in back to protect the neck. Hammers or axes were virtually the only weapons that could penetrate this remarkable defense.

Physically and spiritually, the head is one of our most vulnerable areas. If the devil can influence our mind with his lies, he can begin to control and destroy the whole person. He will attempt to give us a *divided* mind (Joshua 24:14–15; James 1:8), a *deceived* mind (2 Corinthians 11:3), a *doubtful* mind (Luke 12:24, Romans 8:32), and a *discouraged* mind (Psalm 38:8). Yet when we put our trust in the assurance of our salvation, our minds are protected. Jesus said, "I tell you the truth, whoever hears my word and believes him who sent me has eternal life and will not be condemned" (John 5:24). As pastor and author Charles Stanley has written, "I may feel the impact of [the enemy's] attacks, but nothing can penetrate this helmet. I choose to stop every impure and negative thought at the door of my mind. And with the helmet of salvation those thoughts will get no further."[5]

The Sword of the Spirit

Up to now, every piece of battle dress listed by Paul has provided a means of defense against the enemy. Now Paul gives us one more tool before sending us off to war. This time, it is an offensive weapon: "the sword of the Spirit, which is the word of God" (v. 17).

A *machaira* is the Greek term for this short sword, which had a blade about two feet long and was sharp on both edges and pointed on the end. It was designed especially for hand-to-hand combat. A trained legionnaire could thrust and cut from any position so he was never caught off balance.

How do we use this weapon in our own fight against the enemy? By speaking the Word of God out loud. The Greek translation of "word" in this passage is *rhema,* which refers to the spoken word. It is a specific statement from the Word of God that counters a specific attack or temptation from the enemy. We can put it to best use, however, only when we are regularly immersing ourselves in Scripture. As we've already discussed, the devil loves the surprise attack. If our heart is free, he wants it back, and he won't give us time to look for our Bibles. To win this battle for our hearts, we must be ready to fight, with the sword of the Spirit—the Word of God—in hand.

THE FIGHT FOR FREEDOM

When a group of angry and idealistic citizens in the American colonies decided to throw off the oppressive shackles of their English rulers in the 1700s, they soon learned that freedom was a condition to be cherished—and that it came at a price. During the Revolutionary War, many men and women gave their lives so that a new nation could be born. Today, freedom is no less valuable, and no less costly. Men and women around the world continue to make the ultimate sacrifice so that others may enjoy the fruits of a life of freedom. The fight continues.

So too does the battle for your heart. If you are a Christian, you are already assured of the ultimate victory—salvation and eternity with our Lord. But the enemy will not rest in his efforts to make your present life as miserable and ineffective as possible. He wants to recapture your heart. Don't let him do it! We've just explored how to defend your heart and how to "dress" for battle. Now we'll take a look at another vital step toward keeping your heart free.

A Thought to Remember

Most of us monitor the oil level in our cars more carefully than we watch our hearts.

A Verse to Review

"Above all else, guard your heart, for it is the wellspring of life."

Proverbs 4:23

A Question for Reflection

What specifically are you doing to guard your heart?

CHAPTER SEVEN

NURTURING THE FREE HEART

"I meditate on your precepts and consider your ways. I delight in your decrees."

PSALM 119:15–16

So far in this book, we've explored how to free your heart from guilt, bitterness, and anxiety and how to defend your heart from attacks by the enemy. To keep your heart healthy and free, however, requires another important commitment. You must also nurture your heart.

The body cannot survive without nourishment. Each of us needs food and water to sustain and strengthen us; no one is immune to this requirement. Your spiritual heart is just as dependent on spiritual nourishment, which is the everlasting Word of God. Your heart will not stay free unless you feed and care for it properly. Jesus tells us that "Man does not live on bread alone, but on every word that comes from the mouth of God" (Matthew 4:4).

Many of us as believers and followers of Christ go to church. A number of us spend time reading our Bibles. Some of us are involved in Bible studies or take the time to memorize Scripture. The result is that we have an intellectual understanding of Scripture and what God has said to us and done for us over the ages. Yet so often, it stops there. As Alexander Maclaren has written, "We are all so busy thinking about Christianity that we have lost our hold of Christ."[1]

It's been said that the greatest distance in the world is the eighteen inches from your head to your heart. You may *ingest* the nourishment that is God's

Word, but if you don't consistently *digest* it, you will eventually grow weak, and your heart will once again be vulnerable to the snares of the enemy.

We know that eating healthy food will nourish our bodies. How, then, should we nurture our hearts? The best way I know is through an oft-forgotten practice: meditation.

MEDITATION ROOTS

We live in a hurried and harried world. The twenty-first century offers instant coffee and instant messaging, telecommuting and teleconferencing, fast tracks and fast food. We're a people with too much to do and too little time to do it. I read a story that illustrates what's happening to many of us:

> A friend was running around the kitchen with her cell phone in hand, trying to heat leftovers in the microwave to eat in the car on the way to a meeting she was already late for. Her home phone rang, and the answering machine started blaring, just as she was dialing her cell phone to tell the people she was meeting she was running late. The only problem was that instead of dialing the number on the phone in her hand, she had punched it into the microwave keypad![2]

In this pell-mell environment, if we stop for more than a few moments to think about something, we feel guilty since we're not "accomplishing" anything. To many people, the idea of meditation sounds old-fashioned and a waste of time.

Others see meditation as unbiblical. It reminds them of Hindu mantras or New Age techniques. In truth, however, Bible-style meditation is a time-honored method of study and worship. God's people have always been instructed to reflect on His commands: "Do not let this Book of the Law depart from your mouth; meditate on it day and night" (Joshua 1:8). It is a practice that is more than drudgery or duty. It should bring us joy: "[A man's] delight is in the law of the LORD, and on his law he meditates day and night" (Psalm 1:2).

Many people confuse meditation with memorization. There is certainly value in committing Scripture to memory. It is a way of planting Scripture in our minds that can be recalled and used for enlightenment or encouragement on a moment's notice. But those "memory roots" do not go very deep. A sudden hardship—a "storm"—may render them ineffective and wash those roots away. Meditation is a process that enables Scripture to take root not only in our minds, but also in our hearts. By taking the time to understand and incorporate God's Word throughout our being, we are nourishing our heart. These "meditation roots" reach down so far that they will never be removed. They become powerful and effective.

Andrew Murray has written:

"I am convinced that one chief cause why some do not grow more in grace is that they do not take time to hold converse with the Lord in secret. Spiritual, divine truth does not thus become our possession at once. Although I understand what I read, although I consent heartily to it, although I receive it, it may speedily fade away and be forgotten, unless by private meditation I give it time to become fixed and rooted in me, to become united and identified with me."[3]

Meditation is an effective way to avoid the disconnect between a head full of Scripture and a heart full of sin. The Pharisees knew the facts of Scripture and were experts in doctrine, yet all their study of the Old Testament didn't change their lives. They still oppressed the poor, defrauded widows, and pursued shady business practices (Matthew 23:1–36). There was no heart application.

Author and theology professor Howard Hendricks has observed, "You can get mentally excited by the truth, yet fail to be morally changed by it."[4] Meditation is the plow that breaks up the fallow ground (Jeremiah 4:3; Hosea 10:12). It enables you to rebuild your thought structures, refocus your emotions, and redirect your will. It removes the old thinking and attitudes and replaces them with God's truth.

Years ago, I got a lesson on the power of meditation from a member of my first congregation, in a small church in Carver, Oregon. There was a woman there we all called "Grandma Hoyt." She was the portrait of everyone's grandmother: gray hair, glasses, a little plump, and the sweetest smile and personality this side of the Rocky Mountains. I sensed that she and the Lord had a special relationship. I had the feeling nothing could faze her.

One Sunday I challenged my congregation to choose a verse they were already very familiar with and meditate on it each day for the following week. I didn't know who would take up my challenge or what the impact would be, but I believed there had to be someone who would benefit from an encounter with meditation. To my surprise, right after the next Sunday service, Grandma Hoyt jostled past the other worshipers to greet me at the front of the sanctuary. Her smile was extra bright that morning.

"You know, Pastor," she said, "when I was a young girl, we always concluded our Sunday school classes by reciting Psalm 19:14 together: 'May the words of my mouth and the meditation of my heart be pleasing in your sight, O LORD, my Rock and my Redeemer.' Every Sunday it was the same thing. But this week, I did what you said. I took that verse I'd said hundreds of times and began to think about it and pray over it and meditate on it."

Grandma Hoyt took a breath. There was a twinkle in her eye.

"Pastor, it was the most amazing thing," she said. "The last few days, whenever I was tempted to say something negative or complain or gossip, I'd remember 'May the words of my mouth' and be checked immediately in my spirit. It happened every time. That Word had gotten down into my heart."

That is the goal for each of us—for "that Word" to get down into our hearts and change our lives.

Let's explore in more detail how it can happen.

WHAT IS MEDITATION?

Let's start with a definition of meditation that we can agree on. A dictionary definition might read this way: a form of private devotion consisting of deep, continued reflection on some religious theme. Andrew Murray has described meditation as "Holding the Word of God in your heart until it has affected every phase of your life,"[5] while J. I. Packer has written, "It is an activity of holy thought, consciously performed in the presence of God, under the eye of God, by the help of God, as a means of communion with God."[6]

There's a far more earthy way to explain meditation—it's a process by which you chew on the Word of God as a cow chews the cud. I don't know if cows actually meditate, but they certainly have the time and the disposition for it!

However we describe it, meditation is a process that involves wrestling with the message of a section of the Bible. It means to accept it, as Scripture says, "not as the word of men, but as it actually is, the word of God, which is at work in you who believe" (1 Thessalonians 2:13). It must be real and come from the heart. It is encountering the Lord in order to be searched thoroughly, guided specifically, and strengthened internally.

Meditation should lead us to reflect on four amazing aspects of God—His Word, His works, His wonders, and who He is. Reading through the psalms is an excellent way to prepare your heart for meditation on His Word: "I lift up my hands to your commands, which I love, and I meditate on your decrees" (Psalm 119:48).

Psalm 77 reminds us of both the mighty works and the wonders of our Lord: "I will meditate on all your works and consider all your mighty deeds. Your ways, O God, are holy. What god is so great as our God? You are the God who performs miracles; you display your power among the peoples" (v. 12–14). We should consider His handiwork in creation, throughout history, and in our personal experience.

The Word, works, and wonders of God are designed to lead us to a deeper contemplation of and desire for Him. We begin to see that only He can nourish our hearts: "O God, you are my God, earnestly I seek you; my soul thirsts for you, my body longs for you" (Psalm 63:1).

After reading this, you may feel you understand what mediation is and its purpose. You may feel prepared for it. But what does it mean, in practical terms, to meditate? How do you do it? It's not as daunting as it sounds. Believe me, if you know how to worry, you know how to meditate!

If you know how to worry, you know how to meditate!

The most important step is committing to making meditation a priority in your life. Find a quiet time and place to focus on God's Word. It might be your bedroom when you first get up or when you go to bed. It might be your office. It might be in your car at lunchtime or at a nearby coffee shop. The main thing is to find a comfortable place away from distractions where you can reflect on your life and what God has to teach you. Bring a Bible, a pen or pencil, and a notebook. Take a deep breath and clear your mind of other concerns. This is a time for just you and the Lord. Begin with a prayer and invite Him to speak to you.

Now you're ready. Here are a few more steps to help you get going.

1.   IDENTIFY an area of your life that is a struggle. We've already talked about guilt, bitterness, and worry. Is it one of these? If so, you may want to review that chapter. Are there other problem areas? Be honest with yourself about what you're dealing with today.

2.   SELECT a relevant section of Scripture that speaks to the issue. For example:

> Guilt—Romans 8:1
> Bitterness—Ephesians 4:29–32
> Worry—Philippians 4:6–7
> Lust—1 Thessalonians 4:1–8
> Temptation—1 Corinthians 10:13
> Fear—2 Timothy 1:7; Isaiah 41:10
> Impatience—Isaiah 64:4
> Jealousy—Galatians 5:19–20
> Discouragement—Psalm 42:11
> Gossip—Psalm 19:14; 141:13; Ephesians 4:29
> Irritability—Philippians 4:4
> Anger—Ephesians 4:31–32
> Greed—Matthew 6:19–21
> Loveless—1 Corinthians 13
> Pride—1 Peter 5:6

3.   MEMORIZE the section of Scripture selected.
4.   PRAY to the Lord for illumination. What does this Scripture mean for your life? What is God saying to you?
5.   ANALYZE by asking some key questions.

> Is there a promise to claim?
> Is there a command to obey?
> Is there a sin to avoid?
> Is there an example to follow?

Is there a prayer to repeat?

Is there a condition to meet?

Is there an error to note?

Is there a challenge to face?

Is there a truth about God, Christ, or the Holy Spirit to consider?

Is there a habit I ought to begin?

6. PERSONALIZE the text. Say it or write it out, inserting personal pronouns and your name.
7. DEFINE key words and rewrite the text in your own words.
8. VISUALIZE the text becoming real in your life. Get a clear picture of what God is about to do through your willingness to meditate.

Not so long ago, I was reminded of the power of godly meditation. There was a man who was making life difficult for me. He opposed me in every way possible. I'm not proud to say that I developed a bitter attitude toward him—I wanted nothing to do with the guy.

When I realized that I was full of bitterness, I knew that I had to do something about it. I knew that bitterness was wrong, that it would poison me and all my relationships. I had preached on it many times! But now I had to let that truth sink deep inside me. I had to nurture my heart.

Somewhat reluctantly, I turned to a few of the steps above. I looked up Ephesians 4:29–32, which includes the words "Get rid of all bitterness...Be kind and compassionate to one another, forgiving each other, just as in Christ God forgave you." I wrote the passage down on a three-by-five-inch card and stuck the card in my shirt pocket at the start of each day. Beginning with my morning prayer time and continuing during break times throughout the day, I pulled out that card and reflected on each phrase in the passage. As the days passed into weeks, I felt the Holy Spirit working on me. Like water running down a shower drain, I sensed my bitterness draining away.

The day came where I had to meet my "tormenter" and another man for breakfast. To my pleasant surprise, our time was cordial and I felt no anger or bitterness toward him. Thanks to my encounter through meditation with the Holy Spirit, my heart was free.

There is no precise formula for effective meditation. Anything that enables you to hear God's voice and incorporate His Word and teaching into your life is a move in the right direction. He is the master gardener. When you are connecting in this way with the Lord, you will always find Him nurturing your heart.

IGNITE THE FIRE

Meditation is much more than a quiet intellectual activity. It is an active search for God that will ignite a life-transforming fire. This purifying fire will burn away the worries and sins of your old life. What will remain is a heart full of joy, strength, and respect for God's Word: "'Is not my word like fire,' declares the LORD, 'and like a hammer that breaks a rock in pieces?'" (Jeremiah 23:29).

I can say with confidence that blessing, power, and prosperity in your spiritual life and service will be in measure and in direct proportion to your commitment to meditation on the Word of God. We are told in Scripture, "Meditate on [the Book of the Law] day and night, so that you may be careful to do everything written in it. Then you will be prosperous and successful" (Joshua 1:8); and "Blessed is the man who...on his law meditates day and night. He is like a tree planted by streams of water, which yields its fruit in season and whose leaf does not wither. Whatever he does prospers" (Psalm 1:1–3).

Meditation on God's Word brings us vitality, stability, and victory.

Meditation leads to spiritual strength. It brings us vitality, stability, and victory. It fills our hearts with joy and yields "fruit in season." It creates a momentum of its own: the more we reflect on God, the more our heart hungers for Him.

Yet if we are not careful, this lifeline to the Lord can be damaged or severed completely. As David F. Wells has written, "The desire for God does not appear overnight like the desert bloom. It is, like all life, fragile in its infancy. Like a newborn child it has to be carefully tended, nourished, and trained."[7]

There is that word again: *nourished.* There is nothing quite like the free and untroubled heart. It reveals a vibrant and deeply satisfying relationship with God. So nourish that relationship. Cultivate it. Protect it from the entanglements that can strangle your lifeline. It will keep your heart free. And it will enable you to delight in a moment-by-moment encounter with the living Lord.

A THOUGHT TO REMEMBER

Meditation is the most effective way to avoid the disconnect between a head full of Scripture and a heart full of sin.

A VERSE TO REVIEW

"But his delight is in the law of the LORD, and on his law he meditates day and night. He is like a tree planted by streams of water, which yields its fruit in season and whose leaf does not wither. Whatever he does prospers."

PSALM 1:2–3

A QUESTION FOR REFLECTION

What specific Scripture will you move from your head to your heart?

CHAPTER EIGHT

RENEWING THE FREE HEART

"Hide your face from my sins and blot out all my iniquity.
Create in me a pure heart, O God, and renew a steadfast spirit within me."

PSALM 51:9–10

I know of a man who had everything going for him. He was a military veteran who rose through the ranks, led his soldiers to many victories on the battlefield, championed the oppressed, and became the popular leader of his people. This man was also an accomplished musician and poet. Most important of all, he had a passion for the Lord and was dedicated to serving God.

Despite all of this, however, the man stumbled badly. In fact, he broke four of the final five of God's Ten Commandments. After admiring the beautiful wife of one of his officers (covetousness), this man sent for the woman, slept with her (adultery), arranged for her husband to be killed in battle (murder), and then married her (theft). It sounds like a bad made-for-TV movie, yet it was all too real.

The man I'm talking about was the biblical David, the shepherd boy who rose up to become king of Judah and Israel. In many ways, David lived a storybook life. He was a "man after [God's] own heart" (1 Samuel 13:14). But then—just as we all do—he confronted the unmistakable reality of his own sin. Suddenly, one of the heroes of his people and of the faith was dealing with defeat and despair. David was deeply troubled. He needed to renew his heart.

Does any of this sound familiar? Have you ever had life going in the direction you wanted when you suddenly, for reasons you may not have even understood, made a foolish wrong turn? If so, it's time for us to talk about how to renew *your* heart.

Dealing with Failure

No matter how diligent you are about guarding and nurturing your heart, there will still be times when you mess up. Each of us is human, and each of us is imperfect. As long as we are in the flesh, the possibility of sinning exists.

As a seminary student, I once went to a meeting at a church where people were sharing their testimonies and giving praise to the Lord. I will never forget one woman who stood and announced with pride, "I want to thank God tonight that I have not sinned in word, thought, or deed for twenty years." The only explanation I could think of for her comment was that she must have just awakened from a coma!

Contrary to what some people believe, our old selfish nature will never be completely eradicated in this life. When we invite Christ into our lives and grow in Him, we should expect to sin less and less, but we will never be *sinless*. Only Jesus walked on this earth without sin.

When you fail and offend God, if your sin is not processed quickly and biblically, your fellowship with the Lord and others will be damaged. You will likely experience frustration, anxiety, guilt, and much more. You will feel—as David did after his transgressions and I did after mine—like a failure.

We can choose from many books in stores and libraries that explain how to be successful. It's much harder to find good advice on how to deal with failure. Yet failure is common to all of us. How do we turn that failure back into success? In God's eyes, successful people are those who apply *His* remedy for failure. It begins with acknowledging our errors.

Realize Your Sin

After David's marriage to Bathsheba, wife of the loyal officer he arranged to have killed, the prophet Nathan confronted David: "This is what the LORD, the God of Israel says…'Why did you despise the word of the LORD by doing what is evil in his eyes?'" (2 Samuel 12:7, 9).

David was a king. He could have had Nathan thrown out of his chambers. He could have denied Nathan's accusations or had him discredited or killed. He could have sunk even deeper into his sin. But David knew that he had strayed from God, and that his only hope for renewal was to accept full responsibility for his mistakes. When Nathan finished speaking, David's response was short and sweeping: "I have sinned against the LORD" (2 Samuel 12:13).

No excuses. No delays. In an instant, David acknowledged his culpability in a terrible string of actions that would have lasting and tragic repercussions for David's family. He knew the road ahead would not be easy, yet he realized he had to openly admit to what he'd done in order to restore his heart and his relationship with the Lord.

Most of us do not easily "fess up" to our worst mistakes. Even when confronted, we tend to avoid the truth. We distort the facts. We evade. We out-and-out lie. And we throw up more and more obstacles between us and the Lord.

David did more than acknowledge his sin. He wrote a poignant prayer that asked the Lord for forgiveness and cleansing. Today, Psalm 51 is a model for us on how to deal with sin. It begins this way:

Have mercy on me, O God,
   according to your unfailing love;
   according to your great compassion
   blot out my transgressions.
Wash away all my iniquity
   and cleanse me from my sin.

For I know my transgressions,
   and my sin is always before me.
Against you, you only, have I sinned
   and done what is evil in your sight,
so that you are proved right when you speak
   and justified when you judge.
Surely I was sinful at birth,
   sinful from the time my mother conceived me.

Surely you desire truth in the inner parts;
you teach me wisdom in the inmost place.
(vv. 1–6)

David's pleas for mercy are based on God's unfailing love and great compassion. David takes full responsibility for his sin: "For I know my transgressions, and my sin is always before me" (v. 3). We too should adopt this humble approach to the Lord. God isn't interested in our excuses, explanations, and rationalizations. He knows why we do what we do. But He is a marvelous listener to our confessions.

Author Eugene Peterson has this view: "Confession of sin isn't a groveling admission that I am a terrible person; it doesn't require what's sometimes described as 'beating yourself up.' Insiders to the Gospel know that the sentence, 'I have sinned against the Lord' is a sentence full of hope because it is a sentence full of God."[1]

Confession involves three specific actions:

- Agreement—God, You are right! Scripture says, "If we confess our sins, he is faithful and just and will forgive us our sins and purify us from all unrighteousness" (1 John 1:9).
- Acknowledgment—I have sinned. I am responsible! David's penitent psalm contains thirty-five personal pronouns. He leaves no doubt that he is taking the blame for his errors. The Lord clearly expects this from us: "Only acknowledge your guilt—you have rebelled against the Lord your God, you have scattered your favors to foreign gods under every spreading tree, and have not obeyed me, declares the Lord" (Jeremiah 3:13).
- Abandonment—I will, by Your grace, forsake my sin! Confession involves more than acknowledging our mistakes, then going out and making the same ones again. We must turn away from the old ways to renew our hearts. Then we will discover the amazing grace of God: "He who conceals his sins does not prosper, but whoever confesses and renounces them finds mercy" (Proverbs 28:13).

David's response to the Lord in Psalm 51 is genuine. It is from the heart. It is a plea not only for mercy, but also for help in turning away from sin. This is the kind of prayer God delights in answering.

I remember vividly when God, in an unusual way, answered one of my own prayers of confession and pleas for mercy. I'd gone to a bed and breakfast in the small town of Jacksonville, Oregon, to try to process my recent failures and sort out my thinking. When I checked in, I was relieved to learn that no one else was staying there. I didn't want to see or talk to anyone—I just wanted to be alone with the Lord and my Bible.

The next morning, I sat alone in a wicker chair in the inn's sunroom. I prayed and confessed, but it was difficult. I stumbled over the words. I felt ashamed and worthless in God's eyes. The sunlight pouring through the glass ceiling seemed a false promise of hope.

That's when a large man in a white polo shirt suddenly strode into the room. Without any introduction, he asked in a booming voice, "Have you ever heard of Dietrich Bonhoeffer? I just read the most interesting statement from him. He said that when you sin boldly, pray more boldly still because the Scriptures tell us to come boldly before the throne of grace. Isn't that terrific?"

With that, the man turned and walked out of the room. I never saw him again. Stunned, I sat there and felt myself bathed anew in God's love, forgiveness, grace, and acceptance.

It really is a throne of grace. David found it so, and so did I. You can too. No matter how badly or how often you have failed, He is still the God of all grace. When you acknowledge your sin to Him, He will by His grace forgive you and cleanse you from *all* your sin.

RECOGNIZE GOD'S FORGIVENESS

We've said it before in this book, but for many of us it's a difficult concept to accept: God forgives completely. No sin is too great for His love to overcome. No sin is so evil that He cannot remove the stain from our hearts.

David understood that his actions were inexcusable—but not unforgivable. Through his confession and the prayer that became Psalm 51, he sought to wipe away the awful mistakes of his past and bathe instead in the cleansing shower of God's love.

David put it this way in the middle section of Psalm 51:

Cleanse me with hyssop, and I will be clean;
wash me, and I will be whiter than snow.
Let me hear joy and gladness;
let the bones you have crushed rejoice.
Hide your face from my sins
and blot out all my iniquity.

Create in me a pure heart, O God,
and renew a steadfast spirit within me.
Do not cast me from your presence
or take your Holy Spirit from me.
Restore to me the joy of your salvation
and grant me a willing spirit, to sustain me.
(vv. 7–12)

When we look closer at this passage, we find promises that should encourage the most miserable sinner. Theft? Adultery? Deceit? Murder? God can take it all away. There will still be consequences for your actions, but your heart *can* be renewed. When confession is genuine, you can say:

- "I will be cleansed" (v. 7).
- "I will be whiter than snow" (v. 7).
- "I will hear joy and gladness" (v. 8).
- "I will have a new sense of wholeness and wellbeing" (v. 8).
- "I will have all my sins completely and finally removed" (v. 9).
- "I will have a pure heart" (v. 10).
- "I will have inward stability" (v. 10).
- "I will have a new sense of God's presence" (v. 11).
- "I will have a new empowerment of God's Spirit" (v. 11).
- "I will have a fresh appreciation of my salvation" (v. 12).
- "I will have a new desire to live a life of obedience to God" (v. 12).

When we deal seriously with our sin, God deals gently with us. It is vitally important that we understand how completely the Lord cleanses us from *all* sin. If we fail to realize that God's forgiveness is total, we give the enemy a great foothold in our lives and our hearts remain troubled. We tend to repeat sins we feel guilty about. Guilt leads to failure, and failure to more guilt.

In his classic book *The Screwtape Letters,* C. S. Lewis vividly describes Satan's strategy: he gets Christians to become preoccupied with their failures. Once that happens, the battle is won. The devil is particularly adept at using our past to ruin our future. He perpetuates two lies. Before you sin, he whispers, "No big deal. You can recover. God will forgive you. You belong to Jesus, so you're perfectly safe even if you do sin." After you sin, he shouts, "It's hopeless! You really blew it. There is no way back. You can't belong to Jesus because if you did, you wouldn't have sinned!"

We tend to lean toward one of two extremes when we sin. Either we attempt to justify our actions through excuses, rationalizations, and blaming others or we condemn ourselves with hopeless thoughts: *I'm a failure. I always mess up.*

Neither of those extremes works. The only answer is to confess and accept God's complete forgiveness. His grace is greater than we can even imagine. According to Eugene Peterson, "David's sin, enormous as it was, was wildly outdone by God's grace. David's sin cannot, must not, be minimized, but it's miniscule compared to God's salvation from it. It's always a mistake to concentrate attention on our sins; it's God's work on our sins—that's the main event."[2]

> *God's grace is greater than we can even imagine.*

Our sins are uninteresting and unimportant. But God's response? It's more than interesting. It's awesome.

RESTORE YOUR EFFECTIVENESS

For years, one of my best friends, Rick, had been a schoolteacher in Modesto, California. He had a wife and two children and was heavily involved in ministry at our church. He led worship at services, directed the choir, and often sang moving solos in his beautiful baritone voice. I had great respect for him and for his passion for the Lord.

That's why I was so shocked when Rick announced to his wife, Colleen, that he was leaving her. He'd met a woman, also married with children, while taking a class to extend his teaching credentials. They'd been involved for eight months. Both Rick and his new companion planned to divorce their spouses and marry.

As a pastor and a person who saw a best friend heading down the wrong path, I called Rick into my office and confronted him. There was no denial about what he'd done, but plenty of rationalizing. "So what if I'm leaving Colleen?" he said. "I'm in love with Claire now. God's going to forgive me later. You'll see. God's going to make this okay. It's going to work." He was angry and wanted nothing to do with my counsel.

Rick went ahead with his plans. He and Claire went on a vacation to Hawaii. They drew up divorce papers. They bought a new house and new furniture, and planned to move in together.

Then, on a night about eighteen months after our first meeting, I got a phone call. "Dennis," the voice said. "It's Rick. I've got to see you."

We met once again at my office. This wasn't the defiant guy I'd encountered a year-and-a-half before. His voice was quiet, his head down, his shoulders slumped. He was broken. We sat down and over the next two hours went through a box of Kleenex together. God had penetrated Rick's defenses. The rationalizations were gone. Rick knew he'd blown it. As we read through Psalm 51 together, Rick confessed his transgressions. That evening in my office, after more than two years of blatant sin that had torn apart his family, Rick was restored to the Lord.

I asked Rick to go before the congregation and confess his sins and ask the forgiveness of the church body. At the service, Rick began by reading Psalm 32: "Blessed is he whose transgressions are forgiven, whose sins are covered...Many are the woes of the wicked, but the LORD's unfailing love surrounds the man who trusts in him."

His wife wasn't sure if her own love was as unfailing. Colleen's trust had been betrayed, her heart broken. She didn't know what to do. But after much prayer, Colleen decided to join Rick in marriage counseling. They lived apart at first, but God began to miraculously heal their relationship. God granted her the ability to extend His amazing grace through her to Rick. And six months later, in front of hundreds of people, I had the privilege of officiating at a recommitment wedding ceremony for Rick and Colleen at our church. Their teenage son was best man. When Rick and Colleen repeated their vows to each other, I doubt there was a dry eye in the place.

The story doesn't end there. Rick sat in church each Sunday, but no longer sang with the choir or served with the worship team. Finally, I went to him. "Rick, it's great to have you back," I said. "God wants to use you. You need to get back in the choir."

I could see the doubt on his face. "After what I've done?" he said. "Would they want me back?"

"Sure," I said. "Just take it one step at a time."

So Rick asked to rejoin the choir, and was quickly welcomed back into the fold. The opportunity to sing again before God and his Christian brothers and sisters meant everything to my old friend. When Rick sang, tears ran down his face. Before long, he was back in our men's quartet. Then came the day when he performed a solo, "To God Be the Glory." Once again, the tears flowed.

Rick and I no longer live in the same city, but we still keep in touch. This man who was so angry with me while in the midst of his sin called recently. "Dennis, I'm on the way to the hospital for a knee surgery," he said. "I just wanted to hear your voice before I go in and tell you that I love you."

Rick's relationships with his family and his friends are restored. His heart is renewed. But it all started with realizing his sin and recognizing God's forgiveness. Today, because of the difficult journey he's traveled, Rick is a more compassionate and effective Christian than ever. People listen to him because they know he has seen both sides of life. They sense he is a man who suffered the deep pain of losing everything, of being broken, and then, through the Lord's grace and mercy, discovered the joy of gaining it all back. They sense his humility and gratitude. These days, when Rick sings "To God Be the Glory," people know he means every word.

David's experience was similar to Rick's. He and his family suffered greatly, but God took David's terrible mistakes and his brokenness and molded him into an even more effective warrior for His kingdom. David wrote some of his most powerful psalms after his sin with Bathsheba and restoration with the Lord.

Among them is Psalm 51, which ends with these words:

> Then I will teach transgressors your ways,
> and sinners will turn back to you.
> Save me from bloodguilt, O God,
> the God who saves me,
> and my tongue will sing of your righteousness.
> O Lord, open my lips,
> and my mouth will declare your praise.
> You do not delight in sacrifice, or I would bring it;
> you do not take pleasure in burnt offerings.
> The sacrifices of God are a broken spirit; a broken and contrite heart,
> O God, you will not despise.
>
> In your good pleasure make Zion prosper;
> build up the walls of Jerusalem.
> Then there will be righteous sacrifices,
> whole burnt offerings to delight you;
> then bulls will be offered on your altar.
> (vv. 13–19)

In this passage, David tells us that even if we stumble, when God renews our hearts, our impact on others for God can be effective and powerful: "Then I will teach transgressors your ways, and sinners will turn back to you" (v. 13). He teaches that with a renewed heart, the praise and worship we offer the Lord can still be fresh and authentic: "My tongue will sing of your righteousness. O Lord, open my lips, and my mouth will declare your praise" (v. 14–15). He promises that our lives can still be marked by genuine humility: "The sacrifices of God are a broken spirit; a broken and contrite heart, O God, you will not despise" (v. 17).

When Satan shouts that it's over for you, that you're damaged goods, don't listen to him. God can take your sin and pain and turn them into new weapons in his arsenal. If you believe that and give Him the chance, God will restore your ability to bring Him glory.

STARTING OVER

What we've been talking about in this chapter boils down to this: after you've blown it, it's time to start over. You can let your sin defeat you or use it to make you even more effective than before. Remember that the longer you wait to allow God to renew your heart, the harder it will be to regain your freedom. Deal quickly and decisively with sin. As soon as you become aware of its presence, take it to the Lord. Keep short accounts with God and with others.

It's always possible to start over.

Starting over can be daunting. I know—I've been there! Yet it's always possible to start over if you join hands with your heavenly Father. Jesus said, "Apart from me you can do nothing" (John 15:5). When you act alone, you are destined for a troubled heart. But when you rely on God's love, grace, and forgiveness—and one more critical element that we'll discuss in the next chapter—you will be restored and renewed. You will be ready to again bring Him glory.

A THOUGHT TO REMEMBER

As long as we are in the flesh, the possibility of sinning exists.

A VERSE TO REVIEW

"Create in me a pure heart, O God, and renew a steadfast spirit within me."

PSALM 51:10

A QUESTION FOR REFLECTION

Is there some area of your heart that needs to be renewed?

CHAPTER NINE

EMPOWERING THE FREE HEART

*"Men ought to seek with their whole hearts to be filled with
[controlled by] the Holy Spirit. Without being filled with the Spirit, it is
utterly impossible that an individual Christian or a church
can ever live or work as God desires."*

ANDREW MURRAY

B y now, you should be quite aware of one of the ironies of Christianity: to maintain a free and untroubled heart, you must submit to God. A liberated life means giving up control. You can't do it on your own because you don't have the power. It's like you and your portable CD player. You have the equipment. You understand how it works and know what buttons to push. But no matter how often you try and how hard you punch the buttons, nothing happens. Without a source of power—batteries—the music doesn't play.

Who provides the batteries for our lives? God does—in the form of the Holy Spirit. Our heavenly Father gave us His Son so that we might have eternal life. He gives us His Holy Spirit to empower our internal life: "'Not by might nor by [human] power, but by my Spirit,' says the LORD Almighty" (Zechariah 4:6). The Spirit is our internal power source.

I know there is much discussion and confusion about the nature and role of the Holy Spirit. I don't claim to be an expert on all of God's purposes and manifestations. But I am certain that the Spirit is part of the holy Trinity of Father, Son, and Holy Spirit, and that He is sent by the Lord so that we may be transformed into the image of Christ, empowered to live in freedom, and equipped to glorify our Maker: "You will receive power when the Holy Spirit comes on you; and you will be my witnesses in Jerusalem, and in all Judea and Samaria, and to the ends of the earth" (Acts 1:8).

The catch is that we must *choose* to give the Spirit control. He won't force Himself on us. So often we try to run everything on our own. When we do, it's an invitation for the enemy to attack and push us back into our old, selfish ways: "Those controlled by the sinful nature cannot please God. You, however, are controlled not by the sinful nature but by the Spirit, if the Spirit of God lives in you. And if anyone does not have the Spirit of Christ, he does not belong to Christ" (Romans 8:8–9).

> *We must choose to give the Spirit control.*

When we try to live without the power of the Spirit, we usually turn to two common strategies: suppression and eradication. Suppression is what the legalists try to accomplish with their lists and rules. They try to hold the flesh down by external restraints. This only causes pressure to build up until there is an implosion or explosion. We see it with teenagers who grow up with especially strict parents. Rules alone do not work. As author and apologist Josh McDowell has written, "Rules without relationship leads to rebellion."[1]

Eradication, on the other hand, is what some sincere people aim for. They dedicate themselves to prayer and fasting in hopes that God will completely remove their old nature, leaving them incapable of sin. They see it like an operation for a tumor—once the surgeon removes the tumor, it's gone for good.

God's way doesn't fit with either of these strategies. Rather than suppression or eradication, His method is *counteraction*. It's the only approach that works. The Christian life is supernatural and must be lived by supernatural means. When we consistently choose to allow the Holy Spirit control of our lives, He counteracts our sinful, selfish nature and produces the fruit of the Spirit in our lives. What kind of fruit? "Love, joy, peace, patience, kindness, goodness, faithfulness, gentleness and self-control" (Galatians 5:22–23). Isn't that a description of an untroubled heart?

Here are some examples of what the Holy Spirit has already done in the life of every believer:

- HE REGENERATES US. We are born again and discover a new life in Christ: "I tell you the truth, no one can enter the kingdom of God unless he is born of water and the Spirit. Flesh gives birth to flesh, but the Spirit gives birth to spirit" (John 3:5–6).
- HE INDWELLS US. His presence within us is permanent. You can never again say you are "only human" because you have the Spirit of God in you: "Do you not know that your body is a temple of the Holy Spirit, who is in you, whom you have received from God? You are not your own; you were bought at a price. Therefore honor God with your body" (1 Corinthians 6:19–20).
- HE BAPTIZES US. If you are a believer, you already have the baptism of the Spirit and are a member of the body of Christ: "For we were all baptized by one Spirit into one body—whether Jews or Greeks, slave or free—and we were all given the one Spirit to drink" (1 Corinthians 12:13).
- HE SEALS US. In years past, an important or secret message would be written onto a piece of parchment, which was then rolled up. Someone affixed wax to the edge of the parchment and sealed it with the mark of a ring. When the parchment arrived with the seal intact, the receiver had his guarantee that no one had read the message. In a similar way, the Holy Spirit guarantees that we arrive intact at our destination: "And do not grieve the Holy Spirit of God, with whom you were sealed for the day of redemption" (Ephesians 4:30).
- HE GIFTS US. Our spiritual gift, designed to build up fellow believers and bring glory to God, is given to us directly by the Holy Spirit: "Now to each one a manifestation [gift] of the Spirit is given for the common good" (1 Corinthians 12:7).

Each of these ministries of the Holy Spirit is so vital. Each helps us live with a free and untroubled heart.

SUBMIT TO THE SPIRIT

I've already said that giving control of your life to the Holy Spirit is a choice. It's one we make over and over. The apostle Paul wrote, "Do not get drunk on wine, which leads to debauchery. Instead, be filled with [controlled by] the Spirit" (Ephesians 5:18). The Greek translation of Paul's words *be filled* is an imperative verb in the present tense—a continuing obligation. For the Holy Spirit to do His work, we must voluntarily give up control to Him. When we hand the baton to the Holy Spirit and allow Him to direct our lives, we find Him making music that's more pleasing than anything we'd imagined.

Both wine and the Spirit affect how we walk and talk. One causes us to behave unnaturally; the other leads us to act supernaturally. For most of my life, my father lived "unnaturally." He was an alcoholic. He berated and beat me and my brothers. The words hurt more than the blows. I still remember the time I was thirteen and leaving our home with some friends. My dad stood on the front porch, drunk and unsteady on his feet, yelling to me, my friends, and the neighborhood, "Get out of here! You're nothing but a no-good punk! I hope you never come back!" It was worse than humiliating. My own father was rejecting me.

The Lord has His ways, however. To my complete shock, when my father was sixty-five, a man I'd introduced to Christ led my dad to the Lord. It was a miracle I'd prayed about for years but never thought I'd see. Soon after, I had the privilege of baptizing my father in front of five hundred people.

The changes in my dad were remarkable. He stopped drinking. He joined Bible studies. His attitude shifted from mean and crude to gracious. He became a custodian for our church. One evening I encountered him in the sanctuary, polishing the pulpit. He stopped, put down his rag, and looked me in the eye.

"Dennis," he said, "I want to say something. I just want you to know how much I love and appreciate you. I am so impressed with what God has done in your life, and with the way you connect to people with your sermons and all you're doing at the church. It's really something to see."

I was speechless. It was hard to believe this was the same man who continually insulted me and whipped me with a rubber hose during my childhood.

My dad never could have changed so dramatically on his own. I know he relied on the Holy Spirit. Jesus said, "If anyone is thirsty, let him come to me and drink. Whoever believes in me, as the Scripture has said, streams of living water will flow from within him" (John 7:37–38). The book of John goes on to explain,

"By this [Jesus] meant the Spirit, whom those who believed in him were later to receive" (v. 39).

My dad was thirsty his whole life. In his final years, he at last began to drink from the cup of eternal life and the streams of living water flowed out of him. The difference in those last years was that he gave control to the Holy Spirit. We also must admit our need, submit to the Spirit's control, and commit to following His lead.

WALK IN THE SPIRIT

Someone once asked an accomplished adventurer how he climbed Mount Everest. The humorous yet honest answer? One step at a time.

Keeping in step with the Spirit is the key to living the victorious Christian life. The only way I know to do that is one deliberate step after another. When we focus on His leading throughout the day, paying attention to His guidance and direction at each crossroads, we'll stay on the right path. Scripture puts it this way: "But I say, walk and live habitually in the Holy Spirit—responsive to and controlled and guided by the Spirit; then you will certainly not gratify the cravings and desires of the flesh—of human nature without God" (Galatians 5:16 AMP).

Think about a violinist getting ready to play. The violin is a sensitive instrument. Temperature, movement, and simply time will cause its strings to loosen or tighten. The violinist must carefully tune before every rehearsal and concert or her playing will be off-key. In the same way, we must watch each day that we are staying in tune with the Spirit. The goal is a consistent, positive reliance on the presence and power of the Spirit.

Sometimes our impatience gets the better of us. We want to get where we're going. We think we see the way, so we strike out on our own—and before we know it, we're falling off a cliff and into a valley of sin. Only when we choose with each step to remain sensitive and responsive to the Holy Spirit will we reach the destination intended for each of us. As John R. W. Stott once wrote, "Christianity is not simply a Sunday stroll with Jesus—it is a walk that involves a daily, deliberate choice to allow the Holy Spirit to control our lives."

The Lord is quite specific about His instructions for us—we are to submit to the Spirit and walk in the Spirit. His Word in Scripture is not a suggestion but a command. The implication is obvious. If we fall out of step with the Spirit, our hearts are headed for trouble.

QUENCH NOT THE SPIRIT

Just as there are two positive commands that will empower us to live holy lives, we also must pay attention to two negative commands. Scripture says, "Do not quench the Holy Spirit" (1 Thessalonians 5:19 AMP). This means that we must not suppress or subdue His promptings. I admit that there have been many times I resisted or put off a "holy nudge" to speak to someone nearby, make a phone call, give money, or write a letter. When we sense that God is calling on us to act and we refuse, we cut off that flow of living water and quench His Spirit.

I know of a businessman named Chuck Ripka who once confronted this issue. He was married and a father of four. After a series of financial struggles, he found a job as a salesman at a furniture store. One day soon after, a man walked into the store. Chuck felt a clear prompting from the Lord to pray with the man. Immediately, he felt anxious.

Lord, Chuck thought, *I can't. I'm on commission, and I'm having a bad week. I can't afford for him to walk out.* Chuck didn't just fear losing a sale, though. The idea of praying with someone he'd never met scared him. *I don't know how to do this. What if he laughs at me? What if he gets mad?* Chuck tried to think of more reasons for avoiding the whole idea.

Finally, however, Chuck submitted. As uncomfortable as he was with the idea of praying with a stranger, he was even more uncomfortable with resisting God. He began a conversation with the man and discovered he'd just divorced. The man felt his life was falling apart. It took only a few minutes for Chuck to begin talking about Jesus. Before the conversation was over, Chuck had prayed with the man and helped him invite Christ into his heart.[2]

There are many ways to quench the Spirit. We may ignore His promptings to keep our mouths shut when others are gossiping. We may close our ears to His leading about watching an inappropriate movie. We may resist His urging to forgive. Just remember that saying no to God is never a good idea. Allow His Spirit to lead you and you'll be amazed at what He does in your life.

GRIEVE NOT THE SPIRIT

The second negative command we must follow is not to grieve the Spirit. Scripture says, "Don't grieve God. Don't break His heart. His Holy Spirit, moving and breathing in you, is the most intimate part of your life, making you fit for Himself. Don't take such a gift for granted" (Ephesians 4:30 MSG).

We grieve the Holy Spirit when we say yes to sin. We have to remember that He is not only spiritual and our source of power, but also a *person*. Not a physical person like we're used to, but a person nonetheless—and a tender and sensitive one at that. Our actions can literally bring sadness to the Spirit inside us.

There was a time when our family lived in the same neighborhood as a junior high–aged boy with a mental handicap. My son, Tim, was about the same age. Joan and I talked to Tim directly about our desire for him to treat this boy with kindness and not tease him the way some of the other kids did.

Despite our urging, however, Tim one day grabbed this boy's hat, held it out of reach, and taunted him with it as they neared our house on their walk home from school. Tim finally threw the hat into the street and turned into our driveway. He stopped short, however, when he saw Joan standing at the window. He realized she had seen it all.

Expecting a stern scolding at the least, Tim slowly opened the front door and faced his mother. Joan said nothing, however. She was too overwhelmed with disappointment and sadness to speak. Instead, tears began to flow down her cheeks. It had a bigger impact on Tim than a lecture ever could have. It crushed him to see how much he had grieved his mother. He decided right then he would never tease that boy again.

We may not be able to see the tears of the Holy Spirit when we grieve Him, but be assured that they are there. He is the Spirit of truth; we grieve Him when we lie. He is the Spirit of faith; we grieve Him when we give in to doubt, worry, and anxiety. He is the Spirit of grace; we grieve Him when we allow bitterness into our lives. He is the Spirit of holiness; we grieve Him with any thoughts or behavior that defiles the Lord.

If we think no one is looking and that no one cares when we turn toward evil, we're wrong. The Holy Spirit is right there with us and cares deeply. Our sins break His heart—and our godly choices bring Him joy.

THE BEST WAY

When we allow the Holy Spirit to be in control of our lives, there is freedom: "Now the Lord is the Spirit, and where the Spirit of the Lord is, there is freedom" (2 Corinthians 3:17). To be free means death to our old nature and its selfish desires.

Then those wonderful character traits we talked about before—embodied in the fruit of the Spirit such as love, joy, peace, patience, kindness, goodness, faithfulness, gentleness, and self-control—will naturally grow out of the Spirit's operation in our life as we submit to Him moment by moment. Fruit is produced *in* the believer, not *by* the believer. The Christian life is so simple that we stumble over it—and so difficult that it's impossible to live it on our own.

> *The world is not impressed by our relationship to Christ, but by our resemblance to Him.*

As we rely on the Holy Spirit to empower us to live out His love and truth on a daily basis, we will demonstrate to ourselves and to a lost world that it is possible to have an untroubled heart in troubled times. Remember, the world is not impressed by our relationship to Christ, but by our resemblance to Him. With each moment that you choose to allow the Spirit to go to work in you, your heart will move closer to Him. Learn to yield to His control and you will begin living the abundant life God has always intended for you.

A THOUGHT TO REMEMBER

God gave His Son that we might have eternal life.
He gives us His Holy Spirit to empower our internal life.

A VERSE TO REVIEW

"So I say, live by the Spirit, and you will not gratify the desires of the sinful nature."

GALATIANS 5:16

A QUESTION FOR REFLECTION

Are you submitting to the control of the Holy Spirit on a regular basis?

Epilogue

I hope that as you read this book, you were able to focus on God's grace and truth and not on the failings of its human author. Charles Spurgeon has reminded us that "Abundant sin is no barrier to the superabundant grace of God." Writing about one's personal sins and failures is not a pleasant task. In fact, it is a gut-wrenching experience! For me, determining how much to share about my own life, particularly as someone who has held positions of trust, has been an intense struggle. I didn't want this book to be about me, yet so much of the message emerged out of my journey to my heart.

It took a lot of time and pain for me to see that my troubles were rooted in the core of my being—in my heart. Only in the last few years have I begun allowing God to strip away the shackles that bound my heart and discovered the freedom He promises. Am I completely strengthened, renewed, empowered, and free? No. It is a continuing process, one that involves choosing each moment to submit to the Lord's love and leading. Yet I am making that choice far more often than ever before. And for the first time in many, many years, I am filled with peace and hope.

I want you to know that peace and hope. I believe—with all my heart—that no matter how often you've blown it, no matter how low you've stooped, no matter how much anguish you've caused yourself and those around you, you *can* experience the joyful and restful state of being Jesus alludes to when He says, "Do not let your heart be troubled."

Now that you've finished the book, I urge you to do more than say, "That was interesting," and then file it on a shelf. *Act* on what you've read here: "Don't only hear the message, but put it into practice; otherwise you are merely deluding yourselves" (James 1:22 PHILLIPS). Review the chapters. Ask what God is teaching you with these words. Understand the heart and its significance to the Lord. Examine whether guilt, bitterness, anxiety, or other traps of the enemy have ensnared your heart. Take the steps to free your heart and keep it that way. Dive into the questions provided at the end of this book to further your understanding and equip you to live the life God intended for you. I believe you did not come to this book by accident—somewhere within its pages, God has a specific message for you.

The Lord is offering you real, lasting change. He wants you to experience His joy and peace. His hand is out. My prayer it that you take it, so the Great Healer of wounded and troubled hearts can meet you at your point of need, just as He has done for me and countless others.

> *"I am confident of this: that the One who has begun his good work in you will go on developing it until the day of Jesus Christ."*

PHILIPPIANS 1:6 (PHILLIPS)

GOING DEEPER

CHAPTER 1
A TROUBLED HEART

1. What experiences have you had that indicate trouble was/is lurking in the hidden chambers of your heart?

2. What are the symptoms of a troubled heart?

3. There are troubles that we experience as a normal part of living in this world. We are not to be surprised by them or to consider them strange, but to rejoice (1 Peter 4:12–13). How is this possible?

4. The troubles that torment us from within are the most difficult to deal with and can cause the greatest harm. What are the top three troubles from within that you are struggling with?

5. When you have witnessed another Christian's life implode, what was your reaction? How do you explain your reaction?

6. Read again slowly Dr. Allen's description of self-medicating on page 15. Can you identify with it? If so, what kind of anesthetic have you used to try to deaden the pain of a troubled heart?

7. Are you ready and willing to embark on a journey to the center of your heart? What are your concerns as you begin the journey?

CHAPTER 2

EXPERIENCING A CHANGED HEART

1. What is your concept/understanding of your "spiritual heart?"

2. When did you first begin to get an intellectual understanding of what it meant to "ask Jesus into your heart?"

3. Was there ever a specific time in your life when the intellect, emotions, and will converged and you experienced a spiritual conversion? If so, briefly describe that experience.

4. How has your conversion experience changed your life? What are some of the evidences that you have a new heart?

5. Why do you think so many people who have been converted still experience a troubled heart?

6. Do a self-examination—an EKG—of your spiritual heart using the thirteen specific heart ailments listed in Mark 7:21–22. Which of the attitudes and/or actions are recurring problems in your life?

CHAPTER 3

FREEING THE GUILTY HEART

1. How have you allowed your past to control your present and future?

2. Is there a specific sin you have repeatedly confessed to God that you continue to feel guilty about? If so, why do you think you aren't free from guilt?

3. Which one of the seven traps listed on pages 37–39 do you think is the cause of your lingering feeling of guilt? What will you do about it?

4. Review the three scriptural truths on page 41 that vividly describe what God does with sins we have confessed and renounced. Think through their implications and thank God for what He has done with your sins.

5. Discuss the proper responses to guilt feelings listed on pages 43–44 and commit to working through them with a trusted friend.

CHAPTER 4

FREEING THE BITTER HEART

1. How have you been hurt most deeply in the past and by whom? How have you processed that hurt?

2. Retrace the steps of the development of a bitter heart described on pages 48–49. Is there any evidence in your life that a bitter heart has developed?

3. How do you feel about forgiving those who have offended or hurt you?

4. Describe in your own words what it means to forgive and why it is so important.

5. Have you freely and fully forgiven everyone who has sinned against you? If not, why not?

6. Review on pages 51–56 the progression to letting go of bitterness and arriving at forgiveness. Where are you in this progression? Will you move forward?

Chapter 5

Freeing the Anxious Heart

1. What has caused the most anxiety in your life?

2. When does anxiety most often raise its ugly head in your life?

3. How will "paying attention to the tension" help you in dealing with anxiety and worry?

4. Read Philippians 4:6–7 in several Bible translations and paraphrases. Meditate on this passage and ask yourself if you are applying each part of God's antidote for your anxiety.

5. How does true worship of God help alleviate anxiety? What is your practice of being a God worshipper?

6. Trust and anxiety are mutually exclusive. What can/will you do to increase your level of trust in God's sufficiency?

Chapter 6

Defending the Free Heart

1. In which one of the areas listed on pages 74–75 that Jesus specifically warns us to guard against are you most vulnerable?

2. What steps can/will you take to guard your heart in the specific area of your vulnerability?

3. What do you think are some of the implications of John Eldredge's statement on page 73 about the heart?

4. Describe a time when a "spark of evil" was fanned into a flame in your life.

5. How have you personally experienced the spiritual battle going on for your heart?

6. Do you on a regular basis get properly dressed for battle? Review the pieces of armor described on pages 77–80. Do you understand them and are they all in place in your life?

CHAPTER 7

NURTURING THE FREE HEART

1. Why do you think most people focus more on nurturing and caring for their physical well-being than they do on their spiritual well-being?

2. How do you explain the fact that people can believe and know a great deal about the Bible and yet live in a way very contrary to its teachings?

3. What is the difference between ingesting the Word of God and digesting it?

4. What is the difference between Bible memorization and biblical meditation? In your own words, give a definition of meditation.

5. Do you agree or disagree with Andrew Murray's statement on page 85. Why or why not?

6. Will you begin to nourish your heart by meditation on a specific Scripture? If so, which one?

Chapter 8

Renewing the Free Heart

1. When you sin and become convicted of it, what is your first response (justification, rationalization, blame others, despondency, hopelessness, confession, repentance, etc.)?

2. Briefly define the three specific actions of biblical confession listed on page 96. When you confess your sins to God, do you incorporate these three components of biblical confession?

3. When you have dealt biblically with your sin(s), do you experience some of the same results David did? If not, why not?

4. Review the evidences of genuine confession on page 98. Are you experiencing these in your life? Which one(s) do you have the most difficulty with and what can you begin to do about it?

5. What does a broken and contrite heart feel like?

CHAPTER 9

EMPOWERING THE FREE HEART

1. Do you agree or disagree with Andrew Murray's statement at the beginning of the chapter? Why or why not?

2. Have you ever tried to live the Christian life by using either the strategy of suppression or eradication explained on page 106? What have been the results?

3. Describe God's method of counteraction. Have you seen it work in your own life? What changes did you experience?

4. Review from page 107 the ministries that the Holy Spirit does in the life of every believer. Which one is the most meaningful to you and why?

5. Do you have a clear understanding of what it means to submit and be controlled by the Holy Spirit? Describe it in your own words.

6. Can you remember a specific time when you "quenched" or "grieved" the Holy Spirit? What did you do about it?

7. Do you agree with the statement on page 112 that "the world is not impressed by our relationship to Christ, but by our resemblance to Him"? Why or why not?

Notes

Chapter 1: A Troubled Heart

1. David F. Allen, *In Search of the Heart* (McLean, Va.: Curtain Call Productions, 2004), 56.
2. Ibid, 24.
3. Gordon MacDonald, *Rebuilding Your Broken World* (Nashville, Tenn.: Oliver-Nelson Books, 1988), 155.

Chapter 2: Experiencing a Changed Heart

1. Ravi Zacharias, *Deliver Us From Evil* (Dallas, Texas: Word Publishing, 1996), 175.
2. Allen, *In Search of the Heart*, 7.

Chapter 3: Freeing the Guilty Heart

1. Rick Warren, *The Purpose-Driven Life* (Grand Rapids, Mich.: Zondervan, 2002), 27–28.
2. Steve Halliday and William Travis, *How Great Thou Art* (Sisters, Ore.: Multnomah Publishers, Inc., 1999), 198; adapted from Jerry Bridges, *Transforming Grace* (Colorado Springs, Colo.: NavPress, 1993).
3. Allen, *Shattering the Gods Within* (McLean, Va.: Curtain Call Productions, 2004), 94.
4. Randy Alcorn, *The Grace and Truth Paradox* (Sisters, Ore.: Multnomah Publishers, Inc., 2003), 84.

Chapter 4: Freeing the Bitter Heart

1. David Seamands, *Healing of Memories* (Wheaton, Ill.: Victor Books, 1985), 152.
2. Allen, *Shattering the Gods Within*, 161.
3. C. S. Lewis, "On Forgiveness," *The Weight of Glory*, as shown on http://wordincarnate.blogspot.com/2006/07/lewis-on-forgiveness.html (accessed 9 April 2008).
4. Neil T. Anderson and Charles Mylander, *The Christ-Centered Marriage* (Ventura, Calif.: Gospel Light/Regal Books, 1996).

5. Corrie ten Boom with John and Elizabeth Sherrill, *The Hiding Place* (Chappaqua, NY: Chosen Books, 1984).

Chapter 5: Freeing the Anxious Heart

1. "Don't Worry Be Happy," as reported on http://202.6.52.14/articles/3693.htm (accessed 22 April 2008).
2. Anne G. Perkins, "Medical Costs," *Harvard Business Review* 72, no. 6 (November/December 1994), 12.
3. Anxiety Disorders Association of America, http://www.adaa.org/aboutadaa/articles/revisedoverviewofanxietydisorders.pdf (accessed 22 April 2008).
4. Martin Anthony, "Understanding Anxiety: Effects on Mental and Physical Health," symposium at Oregon Convention Center, 24 May 2001, Portland, Oregon.
5. Lori Mangrum, "I Was Panic-Stricken," *Today's Christian Woman*, http://www.christianitytoday.com/tcw/1997/sepoct/7w5050.html (accessed 22 April 2008).
6. Beth Moore, *Breaking Free* (Nashville, Tenn.: Broadman & Holman Publishers, 2000), 71.
7. Matthew Henry, http://www.famousquotesandauthors.com (accessed 24 July 2008).
8. Warren, *The Purpose-Driven Life*, 314.
9. Mangrum, "I Was Panic-Stricken."

Chapter 6: Defending the Free Heart

1. Robert Sullivan, "Pear Harbor—What Really Happened," *TIME*, http://www.time.com/time/sampler/article/0,8599,128065,00.html (accessed 6 May 2008).
2. Thomas Watson, *All Things for Good* (Carlisle, Penn.: The Banner of Truth Trust, 2001), 50.
3. John Eldredge, *Waking the Dead* (Nashville, Tenn.: Thomas Nelson, Inc., 2003), 208.
4. Dallas Willard, *Renovation of the Heart* (Colorado Springs, Colo.: NavPress, 2002), 166.
5. Charles Stanley, *Temptation* (Oliver Nelson, 1988).

CHAPTER 7: NURTURING THE FREE HEART

1. Alexander Maclaren, *Expositions of Holy Scripture* (IndyPublish.com, 2003), 337.

2. Judge Reinhold, *Be Still and Know that I Am God* (Barrington, Ill.: Willow Creek Resources, 2007), 7–8.

3. Andrew Murray, *The Lord's Table* (Grand Rapids, Mich.: Fleming H. Revell Company, 1897), as reported in "The Lord's Table," http://www.ccel.org/m/murray/lords_table/lords_table.htm (accessed 23 May 2008).

4. Howard Hendricks as reported in "How to Study the Bible," http://crossroads.sks.com/cms/kunde/rts/crossroadsskscom/docs/941699776-09-04-2007-18-47-09.pdf (accessed 23 May 2008).

5. Andrew Murray as reported in "A Primer on Biblical Meditation," http://www.preceptaustin.org/a_primer_on_meditation.htm (accessed 23 May 2008).

6. J. I. Packer, *Knowing God* (Downers Grove, Ill.: Intervarsity Press, 1973), 19.

7. David F. Wells, "Musing on God's Ways," *Christianity Today*, 29 September 1972, 17.

CHAPTER 8: RENEWING THE FREE HEART

1. Eugene Peterson, *Leap Over a Wall* (San Francisco, Calif.: Harper Collins, 1997), 186.

2. Ibid, 189-190.

CHAPTER 9: EMPOWERING THE FREE HEART

1. Josh McDowell, "Helping Your Kids to Say No," *Focus on the Family* magazine, 16 October 1987.

2. Chuck Ripka, *God Out of the Box* (Lake Mary, Fla.: Charisma House, 2007), 26–28.

WORLD LEADERSHIP MINISTRIES

Dennis Kizziar is founder of World Leadership Ministries, which was born out of a personal desire to use the gifts and life experiences God has given him to minister to Christian leaders in all parts of the world. He has worked with a number of Christian organizations in conducting conferences and seminars. The primary purpose of WLM is to prepare, train, and encourage leaders worldwide in their ministries.

Recently, the Lord led Dennis to develop a seminar titled "The Untroubled Heart." Dennis strongly believes that in these troubled times, Christians need practical and biblical help on how to live out Jesus' words in John 14:1: *"Do not let your hearts be troubled."*

To learn more about Dennis' ministry through World Leadership Ministries and to schedule a seminar or a speaking engagement, contact him at:

World Leadership Ministries
PO Box 2161
Bend, OR 97709
Or visit him on the web at: www.worldleadershipministries.org

FOR BOOK REORDERS, PLEASE CONTACT:
World Leadership Ministries
PO Box 2161
Bend, OR 97709

Printed in the United States
by Baker & Taylor Publisher Services